DESTINATION EARTH

A New Philosophy of Travel by a World-Traveler

Nicos Hadjicostis

DESTINATION EARTH

A New Philosophy of Travel
by a World-Traveler

Bamboo Leaf Press

Book title:
Destination Earth – A New Philosophy of Travel by a World-Traveler

Book Editors: Larry Seidlitz, Christina Verigan
Proofreading: The Red to Black Editing Company
Book Interior and Cover Design: Poppy Alexiou
Printed and Bound: Bang Printing

A grateful acknowledgment is made to Hema Maps, Australia,
for granting us permission to print the Pacific Centered World Map.

ISBN 978-0-9974148-0-6
eBook ISBN 978-0-9974148-1-3

Published by Bamboo Leaf Press, London, UK and New York, USA
www.bambooleafpress.com

Chapter title photos:

Chapter I: *Sunset at Fox Glacier. South Island, New Zealand.*
Chapter II: *The eerie Guilin karsts enveloping the Li River. Guangxi, China.*
Chapter III: *An Indian drying his sarongs. Pushkar, India.*
Chapter IV: *The traveler-hermit. Jiuzhaigou National Park, Sichuan, China.*
Chapter V: *Turning bike tricks at sunset. Bora Bora, French Polynesia.*

Front Cover: *A photo composition of three Chinese landscapes:*
              Huanglong calcite pools, Jiuzhaigou National Park, Guilin karsts.

Acknowledgments

There are thousands of people in every corner of the world who unknowingly helped me write this book. These "unknown people" with whom I interacted while I traveled have not only given me most of the raw material of the book, but have also molded my being and, indirectly, my writing style. I thank them, even if I will never again meet most of them.

To my soulmate, Jane Kayantas, I owe more than I can ever express in words. However, when it comes to this book, I can definitely say that I wouldn't have pulled it off without her. Her indefatigable help with all facets of the project, starting with sorting out my original writings, going through the writing and editing process, and finally overseeing the actual design and printing, was the single most important factor in the publication of the book.

Sister Michaela from Sky Farm Hermitage, with whom I have had regular contact throughout my travels and after, has been a pillar of inspiration. Her love, her psychological and spiritual support, and her humor and open-mindedness were a constant breeze of fresh air, encouraging me to march forth. Her comments on my first draft were pivotal for my decision to march even further.

Special thanks to Ron Leonard for his thorough comments and extensive recommendations on the first draft. His experienced input helped me realize that the work was just beginning!

I am grateful for the excellent feedback provided by the other readers who read the very first manuscript: Kati Widmer, Tara Gadomski, Linda Emin, and David Rogers. Their thoughtful comments were taken into account and molded the structure and content of the book.

Larry Seidlitz did an excellent job copyediting the first draft and helped me make my thoughts more clear. Christina Verigan's final copyedit was invaluable at the later stage, as were Kim Agrawal's general comments concerning many aspects of the book. Red to Black Editing provided fantastic proofreading and polishing of the final manuscript.

I thank Daniel Klein for his suggestions, and for his great friendship. Ioli Delivani's imaginative input and constant support was most important at the later stages of the book. Our book consultant, Adam Robinson, guided us through the treacherous process of getting this book to market and helped us avoid most traps.

A million thanks to Poppy Alexiou, the book designer, for working within our tight schedule. I thank Lucy Tsouni, who at the very initial stages patiently typed my difficult to read handwritten essays.

I owe a lot to my deceased younger brother, Andy, the only person in the world with whom I could communicate my deepest existential struggles, as well as my discoveries in all spheres of life. Fifteen years ago he first suggested that I become a writer. I wasn't ready then, dear bro, but now I am.

Last but not least, I thank my parents for standing behind all of my unorthodox decisions in life and for encouraging me to be myself.

To my father Costas,
who is the embodiment of
Freedom, Strength, and Love

Contents

Index to Capsules

(listed in alphabetical order)

FOREWORD

By Jane Kayantas

In March of 2005, I was invited to a dinner party hosted by friends in New York City. Among the dinner guests was Nicos Hadjicostis, a Greek Cypriot who had arrived in New York two days earlier from Europe and who planned to travel extensively around the United States. A friendship began that night and developed during his one-month stay in the city.

Nicos explored New York thoroughly, walking in historic neighborhoods, visiting museums, meeting people, and enjoying the wide range of eateries and cafes unique to the city. As a local, I offered an insider's view to authentic New York living and exposed him to different facets of the city. A few weeks after his arrival, he rented a car and headed north to New England, to begin his exploration of the rest of the country.

Traveling by rental cars, trains, buses, and airplanes, Nicos's five-month American journey awakened his inherent, and until then dormant, wanderlust. Seeing beautiful, diverse landscapes; meeting locals in different areas of the country; and experiencing the freedom of travel sparked the idea to extend his journey beyond the United States. He thought of the exotic cultures he had learned about as a boy—the Aztecs, the Mayas, the Incas—and wanted to see firsthand what remained of these mysterious civilizations. He wanted to see more of the world's natural beauty, to try different foods, to listen to different sounds and languages. A strong urge for new and immersive travel experiences started to grow and inspired him to plan the quite ambitious mission of traveling around the world.

Upon completing his U.S. journey, Nicos methodically outlined a first tentative itinerary of his around-the-world journey, which he had asked me to format and print for him, since he did not travel with a laptop. First, he developed a list of the most interesting countries, based on their natural beauty, culture, and history. Then he created as harmonious a route as possible to connect the dots without backtracking and without missing important places along the way. Logically, after the United States, he continued to Central and South America. He then traveled westward to the South Pacific, Australasia, and Asia. The original itinerary that I handed to him in Cayuga Lake, New York, where we met at the end of his U.S. journey, was due to last a total of 98 weeks. The plan was to complete his travels in India, specifically in Pondicherry, where he would study the work of his beloved philosopher, Sri Aurobindo, at the Sri Aurobindo Ashram. By then, he would have lived out all of his wanderlust and, with no temptations or desires, he would have been able to focus on spiritual and philosophical matters that have always been central to his life.

As it turned out, traveling the world was not as easy or straightforward as he imagined. Despite all his methodical planning, his original itinerary was unrealistic given the enormity of our planet and the unique challenges of long-term travel. He chose to heed to the universe's rhythms, and slowly adapted his exploration accordingly. For this reason, his journey brought three significant changes.

First, the journey did not end in India. Nicos's strong will and curiosity propelled him to continue and complete the invisible line he was etching around the world. Therefore, after his travels in India, he continued north to Tibet, Western China, and along the ancient Silk Roads of Central Asia and the Middle East before visiting parts of Africa. He completed his journey by traveling around those areas of Europe he had not explored in detail earlier in his life. By doing this, he essentially circumnavigated the world in a single journey, moving westward from Europe until he returned to his native continent.

While it is becoming more common for travelers to undertake long-term, worldwide journeys, they usually do so with a selected activity. They sail, bike, walk, volunteer, work their way around the world, often taking breaks to return home. Usually the selected activity becomes the primary focus of their journeys, while the exploration of countries and cultures becomes secondary. By contrast, Nicos traveled with the intention of exploring the world in all its aspects, without backtracking or interrupting his line of travel. His aim, as you will read in the first chapter of this book, was to treat the whole world as a *single destination*, and to actually *see* it!

The second significant change was the time period dedicated to his exploration. The original itinerary's 98 weeks became 120 weeks, then 208 weeks and so on. The exploration of each country demanded time, and he could not move faster without compromising his travel method. Quickly, he became attuned to "the journey's voice," which became an important factor in shaping his travels. When he was in harmony with his surroundings and with his journey, everything flowed effortlessly—from little things, like a bus arriving the moment he appeared at the station, to big things like finding out an annual festival was taking place on the day

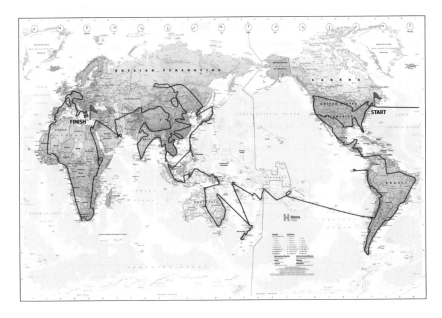

The author's 6.5 year westward route around the world.

he was passing through a remote village. When nothing happened as planned and obstacles kept appearing along Nicos's path, he said that "harmony was lost" and he kept looking for the reasons why this had happened, as well as for signs that it was coming back. He would make adjustments to his day's activities until harmony was regained and things flowed again.

In the end, his around-the-world journey lasted a total of 339 weeks—that is six years and six months—from the 15th of March 2005, when he arrived in New York City, to the 10th of September 2011, when he finished it at the foothills of the Acropolis in Athens. Traveling around the world took much longer than Nicos had originally anticipated. On the map above, you can see his route, and at the end of the book, the list of the countries he visited.

The third significant change was the addition of a traveling partner—me! Although Nicos had set out to complete this journey on his own, he ended up sharing much of his global odyssey with me. Early on, while he traveled in the Americas and I lived in New York, our connection deepened as we kept in touch via phone and email. I joined him twice for a few weeks in Latin America and then again for a few months in Asia. When we met in Thailand in 2009, he invited me to join him for the rest of his journey. I boldly consented. We recognized a soul mate in one another, and I became his travel companion for the last two years and eight months of his journey, which took us through a big part of continental Asia, Africa, and Europe.

No longer a solo traveler, Nicos made minor adjustments to his journey to accommodate me. Our personalities were compatible since we viewed travel and exploration in the same way. Yet, there was a sense in which we were also alone in our exploration. Our view of the world and our travel experiences were not always the same; it was interesting to often see the world through one another's eyes.

While I had previously traveled independently, my long-term journey with Nicos took the travel experience to another level. We camped out on an isolated island, Robinson Crusoe style, in Phang Nga Bay, Thailand; we slept in a floating bungalow and watched the one-leg rowers cast their fishing nets in Inle Lake, Burma; we danced at midnight with locals in a park in Chengdu, China; we praised Allah after surviving a big car accident on the narrow and windy High Atlas mountains in Morocco; we discovered the depth and breadth of French cheese (oh la la!) in rural France. These, and many more unique moments, have been etched permanently into my soul.

As such, I have intimate knowledge of how Nicos conceived, developed, and carried out his journey. Always guided by a flexible itinerary and route, he followed a meticulous method of travel that was built on a foundation of knowledge. Before arriving in a region, he read books and travel guides, researched websites and forums to determine where he would go and what he would skip. However, while he had an idea of what to see, he incessantly asked locals and other travelers about suggestions, never resting comfortably with his own research and studies.

His days were categorized: exploration, study, plan, rest, and errands (see Addendum II at the end of the book). A typical month may have included roughly 20 exploration days, six rest days during which he would also study, two days for planning ahead, and two or three days for running errands. Errand days became novelties as we scoured neighborhoods for a good laundry to wash our clothes, a pharmacy to buy more shampoo, a cobbler to mend our shoes. These errand days gave us a unique view into everyday life and ended up being just as fascinating as, if not more than, our exploration days.

Nicos's travels, as you will read in this book, were also governed by the Buddhist idea of the Middle Way. The reason for this was twofold. The first reason applied to accommodations. Nicos never traveled at the luxury level or at the backpacker level, preferring to travel in between. Neither extreme was feasible for his long-term travel: The luxury level would have been financially prohibitive as well as limiting with respect to the range of experiences he would have had, whereas backpacking would have been physically prohibitive. For Nicos, in his early forties, staying in extremely basic accommodations for extended periods of time simply wasn't an option; he didn't want to relive his army boot camp experience. A modicum of comfort, like a hot shower and a comfortable bed, made his journey consistently pleasurable.

The second and more important reason that he chose to follow the Middle Way, however, was that this mode of travel offered the best exposure to local cultures. Whether he was drinking tea with the Sultan's sister at the Palace in Ternate, sleeping on the floor next to pigs in the Solomons, or attending a classical music concert in Rome, Nicos mingled with the locals and moved comfortably and effortlessly in all strata of society. He even developed his own universal sign language—a combination of Greek hand gestures, Chinese facial expressions, and monkey-like sounds—that enabled him to communicate with people of any nationality. When we later traveled together in Western China, I too began to adopt his sign language and was also able to communicate my needs through pronounced facial expressions and hand gestures.

Nicos traveled with the essentials required for four seasons, all organized in one large red suitcase and a medium-sized duffle bag. On his shoulder he carried a messenger bag and on his belt a cash pouch plus a camera. We must not, however, forget the mini-library, which was packed in a foldable supermarket-style tote bag on wheels and weighed about 10 kilos. Obviously, this was the era before iPads and smartphones, when printed travel guides and a mini-atlas were indispensable. However, most of his books were a luxury (Nicos's unnecessary necessities), as he always needed a context in which to experience a place. In addition to books that were relevant to the history and arts of the region he was exploring, he carried philosophy and other books that he read for pleasure or general education.

This book bag had a life of its own that influenced the journey. On three separate occasions—in the United States, Peru, and Morocco—the book bag disappeared, stolen in plain sight. The first theft, which happened just after he had finished his six-month U.S. journey, also included the theft of all of his American photographs. For this reason, there is only one photograph of the U.S. in the book! Looking back, it seems as if life had deliberately pushed the book bag out of the journey in order to force Nicos to stop reading and start living more fully in the present moment. Certainly, the books were tools and wells of information, but they were never a replacement for real-life exploration. In these situations, he recalled the concept of one of his favorite philosophers, Franklin Merrell-Wolff, who said that the universe's main function is to resist all of our efforts. Nicos's revision was, "When the universe resists, our job is to resist its resistance, and start all over again!" As such, the book bag was recreated after each theft.

Throughout the journey, Nicos kept two diaries. The first diary was a daily log in which he briefly noted the day's main activities—the sights seen and any of the day's interesting situations. The second was a diary of ideas, where he wrote his thoughts and impressions and which served as the foundation for this book.

In discussing Nicos's single line around the world, it is important to mention a personal tragedy that befell his family in January 2010. We were preparing a road trip through the wadis of Oman when we received a call from Cyprus informing us that Nicos's younger brother, Andy, had been murdered. He was 41 years old. We immediately traveled to Cyprus to be with family and mourn the loss of his beloved brother. Shortly after the funeral, Nicos helped to manage the family business and tried to come to terms with this tragic loss. Four months later, we decided to complete the journey, as Nicos strongly felt that this was what Andy would have wanted us to do. In fact, Nicos saw the journey's continuous route from Oman to Cyprus to Egypt (Egypt was our next planned destination before Andy's passing) as a sign that we *must* continue the journey. Nicos and Andy had a magnetic, intellectual, loving, and spiritual bond that transcended their strong brotherly relationship. Nicos's loss was beyond words, and the last 18 months of the journey were completed with a tainted lens. However, Andy's exemplary, joyful, and intense life kept us mindful of a simple truth: Our short time in this world must be lived as fully as possible.

A final note on the actual writing of this book: Nicos began to write it in 2012 and completed it in 2014. In the last stages of his work, I became his advisor and assisted him in streamlining the content and structure of the book. It was an intense creative period where he arduously worked to develop his ideas and to integrate several independent threads into one comprehensive written piece. This process was a catharsis as he revisited past ideas and experiences that were formative in his life. Sometimes I felt he was painfully giving birth to a child after a gestation period that lasted for over 15 years. In many ways, this book is a finale to a period in his life that had been governed by seeking and exploring—of both the world and himself.

Preface

This book is the product of my six-and-a-half-year journey around the world. A year after the end of my travels, I gathered all my journals and notes and leafed through them to find what was valuable and worth sharing with others. Most of my journal entries consisted of essays that were self-contained and were composed on the spur of the moment or close after the experiences that inspired them. My greatest difficulty was retaining the freshness and spontaneity of the original writings, while at the same time binding them together into a new whole: a book with its own character and unity. I first organized the journal writings into themes and wrote new material from rough sketches I had kept. I then saw where these pieces of writing led me. I thus allowed the book to "form itself," so to speak, rather than create an initial predetermined structure to which the content would conform. So, in a sense, just as the journey ended up having a life of its own, the book also emerged naturally out of material that was not originally meant to be part of a book. I do not know the extent to which I have succeeded in my endeavor to create a harmonious synthesis of ideas and writings spanning a period of many years. Only the reader can decide.

I have also chosen to include some photos that I took during my journey, as well as travel incidents that were crucial in opening new spheres of understanding. These inserted travel incidents (capsules), which form the more "alive" part of the book, are meant to be read alongside the main text. They give flesh and bones to the various theoretical or practical discussions. I have also made a conscious effort so that all the specific examples I give in the main text are real and derived from my journey, be it the reference to a Hindu funeral ceremony, the Brazilian Carnival, or a heated argument in a hotel in Hanoi. The photos, capsules, and real-life examples, apart from binding the theoretical to the practical aspects of the book, also provide idiosyncratic glimpses into my real travel experiences.

In this book, I break the journey into parts, analyzing it, thinking aloud about different aspects of it, and exploring ideas as if they were separate, well-defined entities that could be isolated and examined on their own. Still, the journey itself can never be truly communicated to another. Travel belongs to the domain of living experience and is incommensurable[1] with the world of words. As something that is lived-through, it is also unique, personal, and incommunicable *qua experience*. Lands, peoples, incidents, feelings, and ideas may be described in words and sentences. Yet these descriptions bear the same relation to the real journey as a verbal description of a piece of music has to the performed music. The travel experience itself is not made of thoughts alone; it is real, multidimensional, and integral. It pertains to the real movement of Life, i.e., to praxis itself.

One wonders then if there is *any* way a traveler may in fact share his experiences with others. I think there is only one possible way in which this may meaningfully be done: by showing your enthusiasm and excitement for your travel experiences, you inspire others to follow in your footsteps so that they too may have their own parallel experiences. When a person who followed your path experiences something similar to you, at that exact moment you are truly sharing your journey. Paradoxically, this sharing happens *at different moments in time*, and creates a silent bond between two travelers as they have sipped from the common, inexhaustible fountain of travel.

In this sense, this book is neither about the act of traveling nor about the real experiences of travel—although it occasionally struggles to convey both! It is rather the product of an inner impulse, a natural need that appeared after the end of the journey, to *encourage and inspire others* to undertake a similar long-term journey around the world, or at least around a continent or a group of countries. Therefore, I will have truly managed to share my journey only to the degree that I succeed to inspire others to emulate a part of my journey or to create their own individual journey from scratch. Reading this book alone will not suffice. If you read it but do not move from your couch, I will have failed in my effort.

With this aim in mind, I strove to create a *philosophical framework* in which long-term travel may be meditated upon, planned, and executed by current or aspiring travelers. In as far as this book pertains to the (admittedly nonexistent) branch of the "Philosophy of Travel," it does not contain a well worked-out set of ideas and it has no formal structure, since it was not conceived as a "philosophy" from the beginning. It is similar, I would say, to the mode of exposition used by Seneca the Stoic, as expressed through his letters (which I very much admire). The philosophy, if it may bear the name, is to be found in the totality of the work and

---

1 Incommensurable: lacking a common quality on which to make a comparison, such as it is impossible to compare weight (kilograms) to volume (liters); or belonging to another category of reality altogether, such as it is impossible to compare a painting to a musical piece.

in the interdependence and interconnectedness of the ideas, rather than in any rational construction. As such, it aspires to pertain to the ancient tradition of a non-formalized set of ideas that are held together by their having been conceived through reflection on one's life experiences, rather than being the product of independent, abstract philosophical thought unrelated to Life itself. My wish is that the ideas and exposition will also be *felt,* not simply understood. Although most of the philosophical ideas are included in Chapter III, "A New Philosophy of Travel," the whole book may be considered as one long series of meditations or reflections on long-term world travel and life.

For those readers who are ready to undertake a long-term journey, but may still be wondering *how* it is done practically or how life on the move looks and feels, I have included two addenda at the end of the book. The first is an example of how many of the ideas presented in the book may be used to create a tentative itinerary of travel, and the second gives a personal glimpse into the daily life of a world-traveler. I hope these addenda will also help demystify long-term travel.

Finally, if I were to honestly pass judgment upon my own endeavor, I would say that it is nearer to that of a missionary's than that of a travel writer's, or to that of an advertiser's rather than that of a travel philosopher's! Yet, as any good missionary or advertiser must be a little bit of both a traveler and a philosopher, I hope that some of the travel and some of the philosophy (of both my journey and my life) may have trickled through the lines.

Nicos Hadjicostis

Nafplio, Greece, May 2016

Prooimion

Nobody thinks of buying the Great Pyramid and taking it home. Or the Eiffel Tower, Macchu Picchu, and the Great Wall of China.

All the great monuments, all the grand structures of the world, belong to everyone. We can admire and enjoy them for as long and as much as we like, as if they were our own.

Yet, when things get smaller, we suddenly acquire the need to possess them, to "own" them. We want to own a piece of land or a house; a painting at an art exhibition; a figurine, a porcelain vase, and a hundred other little objects. We feel that if we attach the word "mine" to an object, its hue changes and something in its structure or quality is altered forever. Yet the name or idea we attach to an object alters nothing. It remains the same thing it was before the designation of the possessive pronoun.

The idea of ownership of material things is, paradoxically, always connected to size. We can only "own" things that are approximate in size to our human body and its immediate environment. The idea of ownership is just an illusion stemming from small size. We do not think of it this way, because we grow up conditioned to own everything that we can possibly own.

But do we actually own everything we think we own? Do we own, for example, our own body—the basic measure of all things human? Did we create it? Do we know how our liver or brain functions, or understand the laws that govern the way our mind works? It seems that a more appropriate description of our relationship with our body is that we simply "borrow" it for the duration of our life on Earth. Just as we borrow the air we breathe, the warm rays of the sun, or the immense expanses of land and sea that belong to nations or to none.

If we don't own our body, then we may go as far as saying that we own nothing. We actually borrow everything. The things we own proper, the ones to which the word "mine" has been attached—because we have inherited or bought them— will be left behind the moment we die. They too are simply borrowed for the duration of our life. Is not the house we rent as much "ours" as the house our neighbor bought with all his savings is his? Don't we own our hotel room for the nights we enjoy it as much as we own our bedroom at home when we sleep in it?

In some strange sense, the things we supposedly own are "less owned" by us than is the nearby lake. For we have to serve them in order to own them. We need to repair our vehicle or our home, take care of our lawn, water the flowers in our garden in order to enjoy them. Yet, the ownerless lake that belongs to no-body, paradoxically, belongs to all. It will take care of itself for as long as we live and will allow us to enjoy it without servicing it.

The idea of ownership, beginning as it does from the illusion of size and proceeding to the artificial and mistaken division of things into "mine" and "not mine," ends up being one of the great shackles of mankind. But all of us can break these shackles and begin to see the world and everything it contains from a completely new perspective. Travel is one of the great destroyers of the conventional idea of ownership. We may even go as far as saying that another definition of travel is repossessing the world. Each one of us owns the planet.

I own the world! I own the Pacific and Atlantic Oceans, all the great rivers and forests of the world; the sky, the rain, the stars, the Grand Canyon, Perito Moreno Glacier, the Great Barrier Reef. I affirm my ownership of the immense expanses of the Tibetan plateau the moment I set my eyes upon it; I own the carpet of a billion pink daisies of the Siberian prairie while they envelop me as I travel on the Trans-Siberian Railway. I own the shade of every tree I pass under, the song of every bird the moment it sings for me, the colors of every sunset, the smell of the sea, the dancing ducks in the lake.

But my fortune, spreading as it does across the four corners of the world, does not end here. I also own all the great inventions of science and all the great achievements of all cultures and nations. Wright's flying machine takes me from Madrid to New York, Maxwell's electricity equations govern the artificial light of the bulb on my desk; Plato's dialogues, Seneca's letters, and Buddha's dislike of any form of ownership permeate my thought.

I own every city, every living tradition, every great historical monument. I can lie on the grass of a slope in Macchu Picchu and feel like an Inca priest; I can walk in the Forbidden City in Beijing as every Chinese Emperor did;

I am Cheops humbled by the Great Pyramid, but also enjoying it as he never did; I am an ancient Greek at the foot of the Acropolis admiring the eternal cliff; I am a Pope enjoying Michelangelo's masterpiece in the Sistine Chapel, just as so many other Popes have done.

I know there are a few spaces scattered around the world with surrounding fences and a humorous inconspicuous sign saying "Private Property." I leave all these confining pieces of land to all those who choose to be imprisoned within them.

I am the owner of the whole world. That's more than enough.

CHAPTER I

DESTINATION EARTH

Travel is the departure from one's little pond.

It is the bold renouncement of the petty comforts that hold us prisoner.

It is a movement away from the known towards the unknown and unimaginable.

Travel is expansion, widening, opening-up. It is the conquering of one's fears, in-securities, prejudices. It is the hovering above one's life, past and present, and see-ing it in the larger context of the world. It is the fierce struggle against our already formed concepts of the "other"; the vanquishing of our dearly held beliefs, of what is familiar, intimate, cherished.

It is the seed of our childhood imagination breaking open and facing the sun after a long sleep. It is our soul becoming free and unbound once again—alive, power-ful, open to surprise.

The Ultimate University

Travel is the Ultimate University. It offers the most condensed, wide-ranging, and deepest "courses" in all fields of life. It is the only university that brings together theory and practice and harmonizes knowledge with life. It is the spark that alights our curiosity, leading us to discover and delve into new fields of knowledge, from astronomy and archaeology to geology and biology. It is the portal to new societies, places, sensations, and events we never knew existed; it is also the golden highway to the deepest recesses of our own being.

The Chinese proverb "It is better to travel 10,000 miles than read 10,000 books" is more pertinent than ever. For the experiences gained by travel are pulsating and permeated by the breath of human experience and interaction. Book knowledge helps us obtain a basic understanding of subjects and categorize them; it moves in one dimension. Travel is multidimensional: It connects the various branches of human knowledge that are held isolated in unconnected mental compartments; it gives flesh and bones to the world's nations; it introduces us to new sounds and smells and an infinite variety of circumstances. Travel is not only the Ultimate University but also the only one that is *alive!* By incorporating in its innumerable courses the accumulated knowledge and experience of mankind, it surpasses even the notion of university itself. Travel is education par excellence and thus stands above any other institution or method of learning.

Each one of us should know that the gates of this Ultimate University are permanently open to everyone. Anyone is eligible to enter without applications, exams, or fees. The only thing preventing a person from reaping the benefits is the decision to not enroll. The Chinese sage Lao Tzu said, "A journey of a thousand miles begins with a single step." One need only take the first step.

Destination Earth

This is the first time in the history of humanity that millions of people have the ability and means to travel around the world. What was once the privilege of historians like Herodotus, emperors like Hadrian, royal emissaries like Zhang Qian, intrepid explorers like James Cook, or simply the aristocratic few is now within the reach of the middle class.

Modern-day inexpensive air travel, the immense network of highways, roads, and railways that connect every corner of our planet, plus the ever-present accommodation options, make traveling between countries and continents not only possible, but easy and affordable. Thousands of travel books and blogs instantly accessible on the internet make travel planning a breeze. A year of travel, exploring one or even two continents, is now within the financial means of average working men and women who deliberately set aside the necessary funds.

What once took months or even years of preparation now takes only a few weeks. One need not preplan the whole journey or even most of it. After taking the first small steps, one can plan on the move. Any extended long-term journey may then easily turn into an around-the-world journey. With each new travel-bite, the traveler within each one of us may awaken from a long slumber and become transformed into an Ibn Battuta.[2]

Every corner of the Earth has been explored, charted, and studied, yet the majority of humanity has not made use of this. [Don Quixote] Many of us do not believe that it is truly possible to see the whole world in the same way as we travel and see, say, Italy or Spain. However, if we pretend for a moment that there are no borders separating one country from another, if we actually realize that these borders are nothing but imaginary lines drawn on maps and in historians' heads, we may easily come to view our planet as one country, one destination—as the moon or Mars were when we first set out to explore them. It may help if we pretend that we are a visitor from some other solar system, a space-traveler on the way to some other destination, who simply decided to stop on Earth for a few years to see this planet before moving on. By adopting the point of view of such a traveler, we break the mental blocks that prevent us from viewing our planet as a unitary entity. Our planet then ceases to be an aggregate of countries and immediately becomes a *single destination* with a great variety of landscapes and natural beauty, numberless human cultures, a myriad of animals and plants, and an inexhaustible wealth of happenings. We may then call out with all of our might: *"I'm traveling to Earth!"*

In the past few decades, many young people in their early twenties have begun undertaking long-term journeys by backpacking across Europe or Latin America or other regions. Yet, travel need not be the domain of only the young. Neither must a journey last only a few weeks. Anyone can save enough money and plan a longer journey lasting six months, a year, or more.[3] One may choose to travel along Marco Polo's route or explore the Roman World of Hadrian's era; another may simply undertake to travel around Latin America or Africa. Someone else may be even more bold and ambitious and try to emulate Magellan by traveling around the world.

---

2 The Moroccan Ibn Battuta (1304–1369) is considered one of the greatest travelers in history. He traveled for 30 years throughout the Islamic world that extended from Morocco to Indonesia, visiting almost all Islamic countries, plus many non-Islamic ones. After returning in 1354 from his travels, and at the instigation of the ruler of Morocco, Ibn Battuta dictated an account of his journeys to Ibn Yuzzay, a scholar whom he had previously met in Granada. The title of his book is translated as *A Gift to Those Who Contemplate the Wonders of Cities and the Marvels of Traveling*; however, it is often simply referred to as the *Rihla*, which is the Arabic word for "journey."

3 Addressing the financials of travel is beyond the scope of this book. However, Rolf Potts (1970-) deals with the subject in the beginning of his book *Vagabonding*. He emphasizes the fact that long-term travel "has nothing to do with demographics—age, ideology, income—and everything to do with personal outlook. Long-term travel isn't about being a college student; it's about being a student of daily life … Long-term travel doesn't require a massive 'bundle of cash'; it requires only that we walk through the world in a more deliberate way."

Don Quixote

Volcan Pacaya, Guatemala

THERE IS NOTHING MORE to be discovered. Everything has been found. There are no unknown lands to be explored. Every land and sea has been charted. There is no Everest to be conquered, no Antarctica to be traversed by sleigh and reindeer on the way to the South Pole. There are no hidden Mayan worlds in the rainforest to be revealed, no hieroglyphs to be deciphered. Everything has been mapped by satellites. Everything has been photographed. Everything has been studied and printed in books. There are no great challenges to be met, heroic feats to be achieved, journeys to unknown lands to be traveled. All has been done.

The 20-year-old backpacker who strives to reach the top of the volcano, the middle-aged thrill-seeker who takes the sailboat to the open sea, the old couple who ride horses through the wild mountains, the Greek guy with the red suitcase traveling around the world are, in the end, different versions of but one single character: *Don Quixote!*

Midway to the top of the volcano there stand horse-taxis to assist the weak or faint-of-heart to reach the crater. The life jackets on the sailboat are there so nobody drowns, and the GSM-guided navigation system ensures the captain will not get lost in the ocean. Horseback riding is just a gimmick giving tourists a feel of the past. And, of course, the world-traveler, on board planes, trains, and automobiles, is a caricature of Jules Verne's noble Englishman Phileas Fogg, who traveled around the world in 80 days.

Wherever I look around me, I see Don Quixotes trying desperately to live in an epoch that is no more, striving to heroically battle giants that turn out to be windmills, to conquer castles that turn out to be country inns. All of us attempt to transpose ourselves to the archetypal world of heroes, conquerors, and explorers. But all the adventures and thrills of our day, for which we often buy a ticket, are nothing more than laughable substitutes of the images we firmly hold in our primal psyche.

The 20-year-old girl who struggles with all her physical power, almost crawling in front of me, to reach the steep summit of Volcan Pacaya, comes near to viscerally experiencing the myths that nourished her childhood imagination. The modern sailor, fighting against the mighty winds and currents of the sea, comes near to experiencing the forces that the first explorers had to conquer. Both the hiker and the seafarer simulate an era long lost. But above all, there stands the world-traveler, me, the ultimate Don Quixote, who strives to do everything anew by rediscovering, reexploring, re-charting, and re-understanding the whole world itself!

We all yearn for a role in one of the heroic scripts of the tales with which we grew up, or a role in one of the great events of history. We all crave an authentic experience of exploration, discovery, or superhuman achievement. We would like to be Marco Polo traversing the length of Asia to reach an unspoiled China, or David Livingstone exploring the heart of Africa, or James Cook charting the endless expanses of the Pacific. But it is not to be. We are little weaklings condemned to Disneyland-like adventures in well-ordered and looked-after national parks in Guatemala or Costa Rica. We are tragic, or rather humorous caricatures – even more so than Don Quixote himself – striving to pertain to a world we feel is ours, but from which we discover we were left out. We all strive, but we all fall short, forever approaching the heroic world of our imagination, which exists in the depths of our craving but never appears as a true reality in the real world.

> I wanted to be Odysseus. It is this beloved ancient Greek myth of my childhood that nourished and sustained my United States journey. But in the end, Odysseus sat down to rest and enjoy a peaceful old age. He did not start all over again as I did by continuing to explore Latin America and beyond. Here, among the peoples of Latin America, in this beautiful and often tragic part of the New World, where, wherever I go, I discover that the past was always grander, more heroic than the present, a new myth begins to be born. When, in those moments of clear self-reflection and self-honesty, I sit down and examine my journey with fresh eyes, I can only see a funny, little, middle-aged Greek, riding his horse and struggling with imaginary castles and giants that in the end turn out to be nothing but mere windmills. Yes, now I see it clearly: I'm no other than Don Quixote.

The Earth turns out to be the most exciting of all possible destinations. As the global middle class expands, the cost of travel declines, and obstacles such as obtaining visas disappear, world travel will be pursued by a growing number of people. All this, together with the prevailing contemporary zeitgeist that encourages multicultural understanding, will lead to a tipping point, after which world travel will become one of the most revolutionary social phenomena that will define the twenty-first century. This century may become, for the first time in human history, the century of *Destination Earth*.

Extraterrestrials on Earth

The Earth as a whole—this is the aim of the world-traveler. He[4] sets out to explore, not bits and pieces, but all of it. He has no real destination—all places he happens to be in are part of the destination. His aim is none other than to capture the soul of the Earth.

What a pity that the Earth, in spite of modern transport, still remains unknown to most. Soon after we set out to explore the world, we realize that we have been living on an unknown planet all along. Paradoxically, the moment one becomes a world-traveler, he simultaneously becomes an extraterrestrial exploring an alien planet: *We are all extraterrestrials on Earth!*

Every real journey begins with the wonder of the unknown. For the world-traveler, this curiosity is boundless. Every single day he is humbled by the nascent realization of his ignorance. On the one hand, he is shocked to discover that most of his previous assumptions about the world were wrong. On the other hand, he is elated to discover that he need not leave the planet to explore strange new worlds and other solar systems. Here on Earth, on this unknown planet, he is a real space traveler, an explorer of many small galaxies of infinite variation and marvel.

---

4 Gender neutrality, which has become quite popular in the last decade, is avoided throughout this book. When it comes to abstract ideas, switching gender can be very confusing.

*White Island,
New Zealand.*

We all live around our little pond. Most of us "experience" the world through novels, movies, or documentaries, learning disconnected pieces about other countries and cultures. Peeking through a 40-inch screen is how most people learn about our planet, but the information they gain is trivial and flat. In the end, they remain oblivious to the world's essence, wealth, and innumerable surprises. This superficial knowledge sustains the illusion that we *do* know something about our home planet. But it is just that—an illusion.

It is not just the tangible multidimensional experiences that destroy this illusion and set apart actual travel from its various simulations. Once on his journey, the whole mental makeup of the traveler is soon deconstructed and rebuilt. When visiting a place, he realizes that what he had learned about it before was either dead knowledge or had nothing to do with reality itself. Most of his ideas about the countries and peoples of the world, ideas formed in school or through books and film, turn out to have been distorted.

He comes to realize that his schoolteachers never taught him that the Aztecs had their own Venice, Tenochtitlán; that Hernán Cortés had its artificial canals filled with soil and rocks; that this grand metropolis was one of the 10 largest cities on the planet, having the population of Paris at the time. **[Tlaloc]** They did not teach him that the Mayas had cities that were populated with tens of thousands and were full of paved roads and colorful buildings; that they had books and astronomical observatories, medicine and science; that this civilization flourished in the dense rainforest amidst deadly snakes and majestic birds! Most importantly, they did not explain that the Mayas, Aztecs, Zapotecs, Incas, and many other indigenous peoples of the Americas, although conquered by the Spaniards, did not disappear with their

*The Olgas stone
formations,
Central Australia.*

civilizations: they are still present among us, and their cultures live on. They did not tell him that the Mayas make up 60 percent of Guatemala's population. Nor did they tell him that 45 percent of Peru's population is fully descended from the Incas and that another 40 percent consists of mestizos, in this case part-Inca. They did not tell him these things because these civilizations were relegated to the footnotes of high school textbooks, or the margins of history syllabuses.

In the end, all nations stick to their own kind. They learn only about the microcosm of their neighborhood. Only when one begins to study other cultures and see the world through the eyes of other people does one come to realize that the "great European civilization" of the last few centuries is just a part of a much greater reality.

Most Europeans, for example, are educated in schools with systems of thought and maps in which Europe is placed in the center and everything else revolves around it. This Eurocentric history is prejudiced, skewed, and narrow. It suffers, like the histories of other nations and regions, from the universal tendency to examine the rest of the world from one's own center.

But this is just the beginning of the distortion. The Europeans have furthermore adopted the Greeks and Romans as their own. Therefore, they present the passage of time as a clear, linear narrative, beginning with the ancient Greeks and Romans and somehow connecting through to the fifteenth century Renaissance, followed by the Reformation, Enlightenment, and the Scientific and Industrial Revolutions. Yet, objectively, fifteenth century Florence or the Tudor Dynasty of England or Peter the Great's St. Petersburg have very little in common with the ancient Greeks or Romans. All this is an artificial construct elevating Europe onto

Tlaloc

Mexico City, Mexico

TLALOC – THE GOD OF RAIN. I stand at the ruins of his temple on the top of the pyramid holding my umbrella. Of course, the "pyramid" is nothing of the sort – it is simply a bunch of stones connected by wooden planks at street level, since the whole structure is buried underneath.

Torrential rain in Mexico City today. I'm the only visitor in the Templo Mayor, the Great Temple in the heart of the Aztec capital, which was deliberately turned by the despicable Cortés into the center of an artificial state – modern Mexico. On my right is the grand Plaza de la Constitución with its Palacio Nacional, and behind me, the imposing Catedral Metropolitana. And beneath all these, buried under the ugly concrete and asphalt, the grandest, the most magnificent and dazzling city ever to have appeared on this continent: the Venice of the New World, the Wonder of the Aztecs, the legendary island-city Tenochtitlán.

Just in front of me, isolated among the ruins, a small, painted stone statue of a male figure stares at me with penetrating eyes. He appears to be holding a bucket. Is it possible that he is none other than Tlaloc himself, who decided to flood this colorless, dirty metropolis that covers his majestic city? Is he trying to wash away the filth so that his whole temple below may be uncovered – and below it, the whole grand pyramid standing in the center of Tenochtitlán?

A museum guard wearing a raincoat hurriedly walks past, looking at me inquisitively as if to ask, *"What are you doing here, señor? Don't you see it's raining buckets?"* It is obvious he doesn't know: Today the Temple belongs to *me*. And Tlaloc speaks to none but me – through his buckets of rain.

Of the magnificent Tenochtitlán – with all its temples, pyramids, palaces, chinampas, canals, bridges, and plazas – the only thing that has survived is this featureless heap of stones measuring no more than 30 by 30 meters. Yet today, this little space – and its soul – *is mine.* For it rains, and I alone stand in front of Tlaloc and pay him tribute. Pay tribute to Him, his rain, his temple, the Great Pyramid, Tenochtitlán, and the mighty empire of the Aztecs – that *is* no more.

the center stage of human history, around which the rest of the world seems to revolve.

It is true, and to Europe's great credit, that the Age of Discovery culminated in the Industrial Revolution of the nineteenth century, which paved the way for the Information Revolution of the twentieth century. European civilization, with its many inventions, discoveries, and systems of organizing society over the past five centuries, has become a model for other cultures. What we today call globalization revolves around a nucleus of ideas, modes of behavior, material goods, and systems that the Europeans (with their satellite civilizations, such as the United States) have created. A shopping mall in Dubai, a McDonald's in French Polynesia, a university syllabus in Brazil, a nuclear facility in Japan, and a Michelin-starred restaurant in New York all have their origins in Europe. The clothes we wear – the suit and tie for

Huitzilopochtli

*A single Swallow flies * it is a costly Spring*
*To turn the sun around * hard must work begin*
*Thousands of dead * thrown on the Wheel*
*Even all the living * their blood to give*
　　　　　　　　　　　　　— Odysseas Elytis

Mexico City, Mexico

IN THE NATIONAL MUSEUM OF ANTHROPOLOGY in Mexico City, standing amidst several carved stones of all shapes and sizes, my attention is drawn to one gigantic carved stone wheel. Suddenly, the ground shakes underneath my feet, the universe becomes unstable! The movement of the celestial sphere and the daily journey of the sun become precarious. There are no laws of physics governing the cosmos. Everything depends on man's actions. Sounds and images of a world long lost become alive. Let me give them voice!

It is the year 1518. A few thousand ragged prisoners of war from the last conflict stand in line at the base of the Great Pyramid of Tenochtitlán. The prisoners have a glazed, disoriented look on their faces, since they have been drugged for the special occasion. On top of the pyramid, between the temples of Tlaloc and Huitzilopochtli, stands a huge, intricately carved round stone—the altar. Above it sits another stone, upon which the first captive is thrown. Semi-sedated, he tries to figure out what's happening to him. Four priests tightly hold his legs and two others secure his hands, pressing his back against the stone so that his chest may stand out. The head priest, wearing an impressive headdress made from the feathers of exotic birds and holding a knife crafted out of obsidian, approaches the altar with light, delicate steps, giving the impression that he is dancing. With a perfectly natural, dare we say graceful movement, he raises the knife and lets it fall on the victim's chest, splitting it in two. The heart is still alive: *tik-tak, tik-tak, tik* ... With an even more effortless movement that thousands of sacrifices have perfected, he rips the heart out while it is still pulsating. He cups it in his hands, blood spattering about, and murmurs a few sacred words, which are drowned out by the triumphant cheers of the crowd below, before holding it up to the sun.

The sun is no other than Huitzilopochtli: the god above all others, who sustains all life on Earth. The head priest—one of the privileged few to be sprayed with the sacrificial blood—and the crowd below are now certain: The sun shall not cease to move. Yes, the sun will rise tomorrow! The dead victim's blood joins that of all others in the river of blood that turns the Wheel of the Cosmos. The crowd feels proud, for it knows that the Aztecs are the chosen people of Huitzilopochtli with the unique mission to sustain and nourish him in his cosmic struggle of survival against all the forces that oppose him. The Aztecs are certain that the sun is not immortal; he must be constantly nourished with nahuatl—the precious liquid of life drawn from man himself. Without these pulsating hearts, the sun would stop—the daily sunrise is not to be taken for granted. The sun needs the mighty Aztec Empire, just as the empire needs the sun. The two are intertwined in a relationship of mutual sustenance that keeps alive the movement of the celestial sphere, the alternation of day and night, and the warm, life-giving rays of Huitzilopochtli.

The dead, heartless body is flung down the steps of the pyramid. As it rolls, the soul of the sacrificed victim turns into a hummingbird that flies towards the sun. And as the first bird flies to meet Huitzilopochtli, a new captive is thrown on the huge round stone. On the Wheel.

Quechua (Inca) women, in traditional attire. Isla del Sol, Lake Titicaca, Bolivia.

men, invented by the British, and the various fashion trends created by the French and Italians—the cars we drive, the films we watch, even the majority of the food we eat, all have their roots in what we call Western or European civilization.

Still, the world is something much larger than the sum of these parts. Historically, the five centuries of recent European dominance is just a small part of the total timeline of history. There have been great ancient civilizations from Egypt and Crete to Babylon and China. The ancient Egyptian civilization, for example, flourished for 2,700 years—until the death of Cleopatra in 30 BCE. Similarly, Chinese civilization has continued to thrive for 5,000 years. The European contributions of recent centuries are nothing but the latest chapter in humanity's long development and evolution. In terms of achievements, other civilizations have contributed just as many industrial, scientific, and technological revolutions over the past millennia. Agriculture, writing, architecture, civil engineering, mining, cooking, many of the sciences and the arts, and most of mathematics were invented by non-Europeans. As for philosophy, it was not just the Greeks and modern Europeans who advanced it: The Indians created Buddhism and later the Vedanta, two very deep systems of thought. Likewise, it was the Chinese, 2,500 years ago, who first devised the most elaborate civic and social systems and infrastructure ever to appear on Earth up to that moment—not the Greeks or Romans. The Persians and Arabs invented modern algebra and astronomy, while a Moroccan, Ibn Battuta, was the first world-traveler.

However, civilization is not just the things we conventionally label and group together as constituting the branches of knowledge in which school curricula are divided. Poetry is also part of civilization, and no other nation has created as much

*Traditional
cloth seller.
La Paz, Bolivia.*

as China. Whereas the cities of Europe are crowded with the statues of generals and politicians, China is replete with the statues of great poets whose work, unfortunately, is untranslatable into any other language. Civilization also includes the culinary arts, in which the Chinese have been leading innovators for a few thousand years.

The level of civilization may also be measured by how people live in harmony with one another and with nature, a topic that preoccupied the ancient Stoic and Epicurean philosophers but which the Indian mind dealt with centuries earlier through its many elaborate systems of yoga and tantra. Civilization is also the elaborate social structure of certain nations for which a particular religion or ideology is an integral part of their identity. Tibetan civilization is one example of this, as are many devout Islamic nations and even some animistic societies.

To give a final and rather strange example: Civilization is also the extent to which a society incorporates the greatest number of its ideals in its daily life. In this respect, an inconspicuous and insular living civilization comes to mind that has achieved this in the most potent manner: the Balinese, who have harmoniously integrated work, the arts, and spirituality into their daily lives. There are myriad aspects of human nature, and choosing a few to define as advancement or what constitutes civilization turns out to be a convention stemming from the narrow perspective of one's own culture.

The world-traveler soon begins to recognize many of these things, either knowingly or on a subconscious level. He sees that the world is not composed of societies whose only aim is to emulate modernity or the Western way of life. In today's so-called Era of Globalization (a European/American term that has cleverly substituted Europeanization), all has not been globalized. The Chinese have not

*An elaborate
Tana Toraja
funeral ceremony.
Central Sulawesi,
Indonesia.*

succumbed to Coca-Cola and McDonald's. They still drink their traditional teas in their beautiful gardens and dine in their local restaurants that offer hundreds of dishes. An Indonesian youth might text-message on his mobile phone or gather at the town's main square to watch a live Champions League football match on a huge communal screen. However, he will still go fishing in the morning in the nearby coral reefs, pray in the thousand-year-old mosque, and collect nutmeg and cloves every season, letting them dry along the streets of Tidore, just as his ancestors did when Magellan's ships first arrived. That same youth might listen to the Beatles, but every year during the month of Ramadan, he will observe all the Muslim traditions, including the chanting of religious songs.

The world cannot be confined to our mental models or to a particular modern view. Our planet's history extends back in time and space, encompassing all that is and has been. The world-traveler, becoming aware and conscious of the fact that he has been living on an unknown planet, expands his vision, his interests, his studies, so that they may include the totality of the world's shared history and culture. Starting as an extraterrestrial, he ends up being a rare Earthian—one of a few who relate deeply to our planet and, perhaps, even come to know it.

Star Trek

Of all travel experiences, none could match traveling in outer space or becoming a time traveler. Yet paradoxically, the most interesting space travel and time travel is to be found here on Earth! For within this seemingly explored planet, there exist many worlds that take us on a *Star Trek* well beyond Earth's gravity. We may all

One of the many buffaloes killed – the final climax of a multiday funeral ceremony. Tana Toraja, Indonesia.

board Jean-Luc Picard's spaceship, the *Enterprise*, and "…boldly go where no one has gone before."[5]

The spaceship, surprisingly, turns out to be a simple boat! One need only board a boat, wear a gas mask, and visit White Island off the coast of New Zealand to travel to another planet. This planet actually belongs to another galaxy, the center of which lies a little bit further south, on the North Island of New Zealand: the extended volcanic area of Rotorua, with its steaming valleys, lakes, and many other odd features!

Exploring, even with a simple snorkeling mask, the otherworldly Great Barrier Reef in Australia, or even the stranger vertical reefs off the north coast of Sulawesi in Indonesia, is like entering a magical kingdom. Rare natural phenomena, such as the phantasmagoria of a lightning-filled sky during an electrical storm, when experienced with an open spirit of exploration and wonder, may also be considered portals that transpose us to other worlds. [King of Kings]

There are also special cultural ceremonies that are so far removed from the world we are accustomed to that they may seem like they could be happening on another planet. The strange Balinese Ketchak choral dance drama, where men behave like wild monkeys while playing with fire, or the Tana Toraja funeral ceremonies in Central Sulawesi, with their pomp and circumstance and animal sacrifices, make the traveler feel he has left the Earth.

---

5 Reference to the sci-fi TV-series *Star Trek: The Next Generation*, in which the spaceship *Enterprise* with Captain Jean-Luc Picard and his crew travel the universe in order "to explore strange new worlds and seek out new life and new civilizations."

King of Kings

Chihuahua, Mexico

After exploring the isolated hamlets of the Tarahumara Indians and the majestic stone formations of the surrounding landscape, I returned to the country lodge where I was staying. Sunset was approaching, and I decided to go for a walk around the lodge's extended property to relax and absorb the events of the day. As the last shade of orange on the horizon began to give way to darkness, I saw large groupings of clouds slowly approaching. Soon, most of the sky was covered in a gray and black mass of enormous cloud formations, and I noticed a few streaks of lightning brightening the distant mountain ranges. In a few minutes, the flashes became more frequent; weird electrical discharges of various shapes, intensity, and duration began to appear in different sectors of the sky. I could hear no thunder nor feel any rain; the mute flashes seemed to caress the sky and stand wholly apart from the clouds, which by now had stopped moving, creating a stable backdrop that served as a gigantic theatrical curtain. It now became obvious that this was the beginning of a very rare electrical storm. At this point, I asked the lodge owner, who was passing by, to switch off all the lights on the lodge's grounds so that I could enjoy the natural phenomenon without their distraction.

As I stood in the now surrounding darkness, Nature's lightning show was becoming more beautiful and impressive by the minute. Soon, I was completely hooked on the spectacle and even invited some nearby guests to join me—who, by the way, declined, stating they "had seen such lightning before." I found a stone fence and comfortably sat alone, my back to the lodge, and stared at the vast expanse of the cloudy sky. The celestial sphere was now punctuated by an increasing number of extraordinary flashes of lightning the likes of which I had never before seen, apart from some artistic photos in books that I had always considered to be fake or at least hugely modified. Each electric discharge had a main "lightning trunk" from which boughs, twigs, and leaves of various lengths, textures, and durations branched out. Occasionally, many groups of such lightning flashes appeared simultaneously, filling the whole sky; at other times, a single majestic one stretched along the whole length of my field of vision. I was awestruck, dumbfounded, mesmerized by the monumental magnificence of this phenomenon. I realized that I was witnessing a truly divine display in all its glory. The lightning show, the scale and beauty of which no human fireworks show could ever equal, made me realize that Nature's Art is on a completely different level than anything we humans create. I pondered why we are willing to pay for a ticket to attend spectacular shows but so often choose to ignore the free, extraordinary displays of Nature. The answer seemed to lie in our having become accustomed to receiving Nature's endless gifts and, like spoiled children who get many toys, no longer appreciating them.

I then thought, "What if I now make myself believe that this unique light show is not a natural phenomenon but something that has been planned over many months by a billionaire for the purpose of impressing his guests on the occasion of his daughter's wedding party?! What if I pretend that I am one of the select VIP guests who have been invited to the wedding and that I am witnessing a manmade light show that cost millions?" No sooner had this strange idea entered my mind than I convinced myself that the lightning show was *truly* produced by a specialized company that had been hired by the billionaire to stage it for me and some other wedding guests situated in different locations in the surrounding landscape. While being completely immersed in enjoying the spectacle, I somehow managed to faintly keep in the back of my mind the strange thought that the whole sky was a specially constructed theatrical stage with a giant projection screen and that in the surrounding fields there were thousands of technicians with specialized equipment who were all busy working to create this one-of-a-kind light show just for me and some other invisible guests! The "just another ordinary natural phenomenon" immediately morphed into a "uniquely extraordinary human event"—no chance natural phenomenon, but the greatest human light show ever conceived that was being created for my own pleasure. It was as if my whole experience were transposed to another set of coordinates in which my ordinary life became extraordinary. I now felt as if I were a king of kings, the pharaoh of Egypt, the emperor of China! While in this strange state, I was overwhelmed with gratefulness for being alive and for having the honor to witness such an incredible event.

As I sat motionless for the next hour or so, being completely absorbed by this now-human light show of monumental proportions, it gradually dawned upon me that *I am a king of kings every single day of my life*, but I have become so used to it that I am rarely if ever aware of the fact.

Ever since that extraordinary evening in Chihuahua, the magical land of the Tarahumara Indians, whenever I find myself unable to appreciate something special that crosses my life's path, I mentally change the coordinates of the natural mode of my perception by imagining that I am experiencing something that was created just for me by another human or by a large organization. I thus break the pattern of taking things for granted and suddenly find myself transposed to a parallel reality in which I become a king who has been invited to a very exceptional event prepared especially for my royalty. I then realize that, actually, I am a king of kings irrespective of the magnitude of the gifts that Life bestows upon me. Although it is easier to experience gratefulness during grand special events, the extent to which I expand the range of this practice to encompass the more ordinary yet equally miraculous occurrences of everyday life is the extent to which I pertain to this royalty that we are all born into.

An even more impressive realization is that, while we are all living in the twenty-first century, we have the ability to become time travelers and visit other eras! If one climbs an active volcano such as Pacaya in Guatemala, or watches the overflowing red lava of the Arenal volcano in Costa Rica, one comes to experience what the Earth looked like millions of years ago. Similarly, one may walk on a glacier to feel how humans may have lived during the Ice Age. If one visits Fez in Morocco, he will soon realize that he has traveled to a living medieval city whose residents live and work in almost the same fashion their ancestors did centuries ago. And the world-traveler who is prepared to visit a Stone Age tribe in the Solomon Islands and sleep next to the pigs on the lumpy floor of a thatched hut will be traveling to humanity's past. On the other end of the spectrum, one need only travel to Japan in order to get a sense of what the whole world will look like in the future (say, the twenty-second century). It is not just the technological advancements of the Japanese that set them apart. Often bypassed are their social mores: the way they rear their children, their sophisticated and detailed rules of propriety,

Stone Age: A Karo woman exiting her thatched home. South Omo Valley, Ethiopia.

Biblical times: Worshipers leaving a rock-hewn church. Lalibela, Ethiopia

their sense of aesthetics in everyday tasks, their elaborate work ethic, and their advanced sense of duty.

The idea that the Present in some natural fashion also encloses the Past *in a real and palpable way* has a modern-day apostle, David Attenborough. When he created the revolutionary documentary series *Life on Earth,*[6] he actually based it on a very simple idea, similar to the one of time-travel above. He realized that organisms of all biological epochs exist on Earth *today* and that one need not create illustrative descriptions of the evolution of organisms, but could actually go into nature and film the representative species of each of the great epochs that are alive. Therefore, Attenborough only had to approach a volcano to find the single-cell organisms that first appeared on the Earth three to four billion years ago, then to the sea to film the most primitive jellyfish, then feature frogs as the representative of the amphibians, then in a similar fashion reptiles, birds, and mammals. Likewise, just as Nature contains all previous epochs, many human societies around the world preserve elements of the cultures of the past.

But one need not visit remote places or cultures that actually *live* in the past. A big part of ordinary travel already contains an element of time-travel. One of the reasons people travel to the ancient sites of Rome or explore the ruins of Mesoamerica is to somehow travel to the eras in which these architectural marvels were constructed and to *imagine* themselves being there. **[Huitzilopochtli]** Throughout the centuries, archaeological and historic sites have lured educated travelers to

---

6 *Life on Earth* is a BBC TV natural history series that aired in the UK in 1979. It set the standard for all subsequent natural history documentaries.

Medieval times: Centuries-old traditional tanneries. Fez, Morocco.

Twenty-second century: A high-aesthetic contemporary shopping mall. Tokyo, Japan

other countries because these places ignite the imagination and help them to relate book knowledge to the space and time of older civilizations.

But we are moving too fast. Let us take a step back in order to examine Travel in general, so that we may put World Travel and the world-traveler into a larger context.

POSTSCRIPT TO CHAPTER I

A NEW PORTRAYAL OF THE EARTH

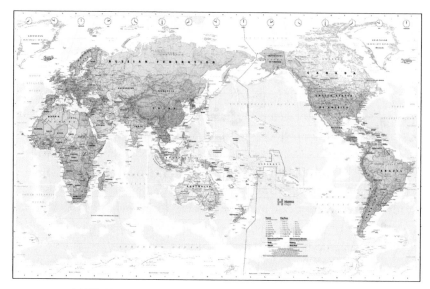

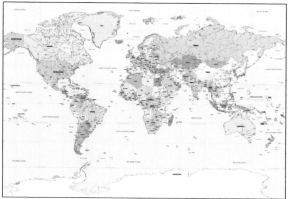

Most Westerners grow up having a mental picture of the world in which Europe and Africa are in the center, America is on the left, and Asia and Australia are on the right. The main reason for this is, of course, historical. It was the European explorers who made all modern discoveries and created our modern maps, so they placed Europe (themselves) in the center of the world and made it the hub of the modern world map—the Europe-centered map. In this map, there is a chasm between Eurasia and Africa on the right and the Americas on the left, in the form of a rift called the Atlantic Ocean, which, in effect, cuts the world into two distinct and separate landmasses. There are many other problems with the portrayal of the Earth in a Europe-centered map, which we will hereby examine, with the purpose of showing why a Pacific-centered map is the proper portrayal of the world.

1. Cutting the Map

For millennia, up until the discovery of the Americas in the fifteenth century, the Atlantic Ocean was considered the end of the world. While Eurasia and a small part of the Pacific were part of the known world, nobody knew, until Magellan's voyage, the Pacific's enormous size. Therefore, historically, the Atlantic "cut" the planet in two, forcing a cultural separation between the then-unknown civilizations of the Americas and the rest of the world. Such a cutting is unavoidable in order to portray the Earth (a three-dimensional sphere) as a two-dimensional map on paper. By choosing to sever the continuity of the Earth at the point where people had "cut" it for most of history, one indirectly incorporates an historical perspective in it that may not be visible at first glance, yet is significant and meaningful. A Pacific-centered world map does exactly that—it cuts the Earth at the Atlantic rather than at the Pacific. The cutting point has a further aspect, which we examine next.

2. The Eighth Continent

The Pacific Ocean, unlike the Atlantic, is strewn with inhabited islands on which several human cultures and languages have developed over millennia. Each with its own distinct character, these islands are related culturally and geographically, and like a pearl necklace, embellish the Pacific all the way from Papua New Guinea to Easter Island. These Pacific Islands are the only part of the world that do not belong to a continent, even if they actually constitute a "Continent of Islands."

It is time to allow this isolated and scattered world to come into its own. It is time to proclaim the world of the Pacific Islands as the eighth continent![7] Its main features: it has the smallest landmass, but the largest area of water; it has the smallest population, yet the greatest diversity of languages and the greatest geographical extension; it is the most isolated and distant region, yet quite possibly the most in-

---

7 The division of the world into continents is arbitrary. There is no reason for one to draw the line between Europe and Asia, or cut Africa at the Suez Canal, or consider Australia a continent but not Greenland. In spite of this arbitrariness, various historical, cultural, and geological reasons are put forth to explain the already existing division. Similarly, through arguments, the case is made here for the introduction of the eighth continent. Concerning the number "eight": The way continents are counted differs from country to country. In the English-speaking world as well as in many other countries such as China and India, the number of continents is considered to be seven (Asia, North America, South America, Africa, Europe, Australia, Antarctica). In all Spanish-speaking countries as well as in a number of other countries, North and South America are considered as one, so there are six continents. Here the first scheme is used.

timate and friendly. If the map must be cut at some point so that the globe may be portrayed on a two-dimensional surface, is it not better to cut it at the uninhabited and featureless Atlantic rather than breaking the continuity of this unique eighth continent?

3. The Pacific as the Earth's Protagonist

It is not just the issue of the broken continuity of the Pacific Islands and cultures; the central significance of the Pacific Ocean itself is also lost on a Europe-centered Map. The Pacific Ocean is actually the single most important natural feature of our planet. First of all, it comprises 32 percent of the Earth's surface—it is actually three times larger than Asia, our largest continent, and larger than all of the Earth's land area combined![8] When one takes into account the fact that 70 percent of the Earth's surface is covered by water, the Pacific may be said to be not just the symbol of the Earth itself, but actually its defining feature. It is because of the Pacific that our "blue planet" looks blue from space. The immense size of the Pacific and the significance of the Earth's water mass relative to its landmass can only become clearly visible on a map in which the actual Pacific is in the center. What would be more appropriate, then, than to have the main feature and element of our planet—its water—be the central figure in the portrayal of the Earth?

4. The Continuity of the Earth's Landmass

On a Pacific-centered map, it immediately becomes obvious not only that the American continent is the natural extension of Eurasia—almost touching it at the Bering Strait—but that all of the continents of the world, with the exception of Australia and Antarctica, constitute one contiguous landmass beginning in Cape Town in South Africa and ending in the Tierra del Fuego in Argentina! This fact is completely lost on a Europe-centered map. The Americas and Eurasia are not separated by the Atlantic, but are actually connected at the Bering Strait. The most prevalent anthropological theory about how humans first arrived in the Americas is that they migrated across the Bering Strait, which was covered by ice during the last glacial period around 15,000 years ago. The 80 kilometers between the two continents at the strait was then traversable by foot. Incidentally, there are plans to create a tunnel (like the Channel Tunnel in Europe) connecting Russia to Alaska in the near future. Such a structure would restore the Ice Age continuity of the planet's landmass.

---

8 The reason this is not immediately obvious on a map is that the northern landmasses of Russia, Canada, and Greenland are distorted and look much larger. For example, although Canada is the same size as the United States, it looks twice as big.

The stone Moai at Ahu Tongariki. Easter Island, Chile.

5. Pangaea and the Unity of the Earth's Landmass

The reason that Eurasia and America touch one another is not coincidental; there is an important geological explanation. All of today's separate landmasses of the Earth used to be part of a single big landmass until 200 million years ago, when they began to split apart and move away from one another. This immense Pangaea (from the Greek, meaning "all-Earth") was the original supercontinent from which all continents were later formed by an act of separation. It is also the reason why the west coast of Africa seems to fit into the east coast of South America like a jigsaw puzzle, just as the east coast of Asia fits into the west coast of the Americas. Only on a Pacific-centered map can the unity of the planet's landmass be understood. One can almost mentally reassemble Pangaea when looking at the map.

6. Change of Perspective

Another important feature of our planet is also completely lost on a Europe-centered map: the structure of the continents in relationship to the oceans. This is very obvious on the Pacific-centered map. One can see that although Asia and America touch one another at their northernmost parts, they rapidly recede along their southern coasts. This extraordinary strange "movement," which resembles the motion of two identical magnets repelling one another, is what has created the chasm that forms the Pacific Ocean. The Pacific is actually delineated by the eastern coast of Asia and the western coast of the Americas. All the regions lying along this boundary recently came to be termed the Pacific Rim.

When glancing at a map, all of us have learned to concentrate on the usually colorful landmasses, with their countries and cities. We see these masses—Africa, Australia, America—as being defined and formed by the seas that envelop them. We see the planet as having objects on a featureless background. These objects are the landmasses while the background is the uniformly blue and featureless sea. We might as well have colored the oceans white, leaving them out altogether! Yet, if through a conscious effort, a person mentally shifts his *visual perspective*, he may actually come to *see for the first time* that the Pacific is larger than any continent on the planet. As in the optical trick where an image can be seen as being a vase or being two faces, the landmasses move from the foreground to the background. It is through such an exercise that a good geography teacher in a future school may encourage his students' imaginations to help them grasp not only the true magnitude and relations of the Earth's various features but also the extent to which our planet is basically water, with a bit of land here and there.

This consummate understanding of the *oneness* of our planet—not only the unity of its continents, but also the interdependence of the landmasses and vast bodies of water—is possible only through the change of perspective that a Pacific-centered map can bring. This is the final, and possibly the strongest, argument in favor of making the Pacific-centered map our standard portrayal of the Earth.

CHAPTER II

WORLD TRAVEL

There is a widespread belief among people who do not travel that it is not neces-sary to actually visit other countries because one can get a good sense of them by watching travel programs, leafing through magazines, or reading travel-inspired books. A new species of "armchair-travelers" who sit in front of their television sets watching travel documentaries has emerged in the last decades. This suggests that it is possible to travel without departing from one's home! The underlying presupposition is that travel is *seeing* places, and that instead of actually *going* to places one may bring them into one's living room.

This mistaken view has to be firmly debunked. The relationship between taking a cruise along the Li River in China and experiencing the otherworldly landscape of the Guilin karsts enveloping the boat—full of fellow Chinese travel-ers—and the watching of a film about Guilin is akin to the relationship between seeing a photo of a person you love and having the actual person next to you. The

*Rice fields outside
Xijiang village.
Guizhou, China.*

visual portrayal of a place, whether it be a photo or a movie, as well as any verbal description of it, are incommensurable with the immersive living experience. There is no comparison between Guilin-the-photo and Guilin-the-place-and-experience. Another analogy is comparing the photo of a French cheese platter with eating the real cheeses. One is dead, the other alive. The real cheeses have a wealth of smells, textures, and tastes; the photo is a mere representation. Often, modern man lives in his mind and forgets that Guilin is a real place situated in a three-dimensional universe with a sky above it, a real river running through it, and surrounding rice fields with farmers tending them. No digital reproduction or literary description, however good or poetic, can replace the feeling of a breeze on one's face or the little droplets from the river's spray. At best, any description is a pointer to what one may experience if one gets off the couch and sets out to discover the actual place.

The Four Types of Travel

Not all travel is the same. Travel may actually be divided into four types or dimensions.[9] Every country, every culture, can be experienced on many levels. These

---

9 The concept of dimensions is connected with that of "degrees of freedom" in mathematics—a great coincidence that proves to be very useful. The degrees of freedom measure the number of axes in which a body is free to move. In a sense, the more dimensions used to describe a type of travel, the more degrees of freedom there are for the traveler, i.e., he is more free to explore. The analogy may even go further: The more dimensions a type of travel has, the more dimensions of the foreign culture the traveler will come to experience.

Himeji Shogun Castle with surrounding manicured gardens. Hyogo, Japan.

levels may be said to correspond to different dimensions of Being. For example, Japan is not only the actual place that we experience in the present moment. In order to deeply relate to Japan, one needs to know its history, the way its culture developed; one must create the time to study, ask questions, and interact with locals. One may also devote time to visit a Zen monastery, a Shogun castle, a Shinto temple, a kaiseki restaurant. The more time one devotes to these, the more dimensions of the Japanese culture will begin to unfold. The traveler will soon start seeing the world through Japanese eyes, so to speak, and start to feel what it means to be Japanese.

Let us examine these four types of travel.

1. One-Dimensional Travel (Point or Line Travel)

One-dimensional travel is the most common and widespread mode of travel. This is point travel or travel along a preplanned and unalterable line. It involves moving from one point to another, usually within a city or from city to city, or seeing a number of highlights in various locations. There is no substantive contact with the culture or locals. The emphasis is usually on important tourist sites or superficial and brief set-encounters with stereotypical elements of a culture.

This type of "travel" is actually unworthy of the name. It has the semblance and structure of travel, but it is not real travel. Having the world pass by while one watches a movie at home, or having a tour bus drive through a country, permitting a brief one-dimensional superficial acquaintance from the comfort of a seat, are actually one and the same thing. Enclosed in a protective bubble, the visitor is cut off from the rain, the sounds, the smells, the natural human interactions of a pulsating, living world. The country remains at a cold distance, like cinematic sequences of a foreign movie in a language that is incomprehensible.

We may call this mode of traveling "touristic," with at least some of the derogatory ideas associated with the term. The tourist seeks immediate gratification and entertainment. He most often travels in groups or joins others for excursions, sleeps in hotels with creature comforts, and has a fixed and inflexible prearranged itinerary with an unalterable date of return home. His main interest is to visit major sites in order to be photographed there, or to attend special cultural events, often especially created for the tourist industry. It is difficult, if not impossible, for him to immerse himself in the foreign culture or delve into the actual realities of the country beyond the display window that has been set up by the travel industry. Above all, the tourist returns home the same person he left.

There is nothing inherently wrong with one-dimensional travel, *provided* that there is an awareness that it does not constitute real travel. Without such an awareness, one may follow this mode of travel for the rest of one's life thinking that this is the only way to travel.

Examples of this type of travel are short business trips or a three to four day exploration of a city with a group. Consider, for example, a 10-day Classic Central Europe tour, involving Budapest, Vienna, and Prague, that might also include hurried half-day excursions to Bratislava or the Schönbrunn Palace.

2. Two-Dimensional Travel (Surface Travel)

This is the simplest type of travel. It may be likened to moving on a two-dimensional surface. The word "surface" relates to "superficial," so we may say this is the simplest and a rather superficial type of travel. It involves experiencing a culture by incorporating disconnected random bits and pieces chosen by a tour operator or a travel agency. This type of travel may also be independent, but the itinerary still remains predetermined, rigid, and inflexible. The traveler does not, however, only move between points or along a limited line. He may have time to explore on his own and have the freedom to pursue special interests or to change course. Still, this "surface travel" allows only for a first taste, a light acquaintance with the foreign culture.

An example of two-dimensional travel is a two-week trip to the South of France, with all hotels already booked. Such a trip would involve exploration of the countryside and villages, as well as important towns like Avignon or Arles. The planning may have been done with the help of a travel agency that organized everything. There is not much flexibility and the itinerary is difficult to change. The independent traveler will get to see the South of France and may become acquainted with local culture by interacting with villagers and visiting farmers' markets, yet there will always be an underlying feeling of something incomplete.

3. Three-Dimensional Travel (Solid Travel)

Three-dimensional travel aims at truly exploring the many dimensions of a region. It is the independent traveler moving along a line that he drew on a map after study and thoughtful consideration. The itinerary is almost always flexible, allowing for adaptations to the original plan, based on discoveries and observations made "in the field." A rule of thumb is that for a journey to be three-dimensional it must be of at least three weeks' duration! To delve deep into the foreign culture, studying and planning is necessary before one departs. Only a small part of the journey may be prearranged (for example, the flights to and from the country), allowing oneself much freedom to explore the foreign country or area.

Long-term independent travel that lasts anywhere between three weeks and a few months falls into this category. For instance, a three-month exploration of South America by bus and car involving four countries would be considered solid travel. Three-dimensional travel would also be a two-month exploration of France or Italy by car, exploring the countryside, visiting important sites and monuments, and also interacting with locals at a deeper level by visiting farmers' markets.

4. Four-Dimensional Travel (Total Travel)

Four-dimensional travel is travel par excellence. This type of travel aims at delving deep into the soul of a country. It is uncompromising in its demands and involves as much hardship as good times. It is never a "holiday," as many people often think. It involves studious planning, working alone for hours every day, figuring out transport, food, accommodation, and constantly dealing with a myriad of problems, big and small. Above all, it involves struggling with the culture in order to better understand it. All aspects of the foreign land become the object of one's exploration. This requires the courage to delve into the unpleasant elements too. Many of these things are often tiring and exhausting. This type of travel is *real work*.

Four-dimensional travel may also involve the planning and execution of difficult "little expeditions" into remote areas that have been untouched by tourism or even modernity. There is a constant mindfulness involved, a continuous striving to understand that which seems to be remote and mysterious. The journey is open-ended, without a set date of completion. The traveler is always ready to restructure and replan his journey, so as to adapt it to his new understanding of the foreign land, which almost always turns out to be different from the one he had envisioned before he departed. Although an overall itinerary might be in place, it is not binding: It serves only as a rough guide.

The four-dimensional journey is much longer in duration and usually involves more than one country. This is travel with infinite degrees of freedom. It

An extended family of the Kwaio tribe. Central Malaita, Solomon Islands.

opens up a whole new universe of sights, sounds, smells, but also new ways of seeing the world and of understanding mankind in general and oneself in particular.

Examples of total travel are a nine-month journey around Latin America or a six-month journey in West Africa, where one will basically be on one's own and discover his way around as he moves. Of course, all vagabonding[10] also belongs in this category.

World Travel

Traveling around the world is a special case of four-dimensional travel. It is the most ambitious and all-encompassing type of travel and belongs to a category of its own. The *whole* of life becomes the field of exploration of the world-traveler. His journey embraces the whole spectrum of experiences—from the simplest and most ordinary to the most complex and extraordinary. Nothing is either too small or petty so as to be rejected, or too sophisticated or "upper-class" to be avoided. He strives to get as complete a picture as possible of the country and society he is immersed in, and no such completeness is possible if he limits his field of exploration to either the elements that are easily accessible (financially, physically, or time-wise) or that reflect his own limited interests.

---

10 Vagabonding: Wandering about with no destination and without a set date of arrival anywhere. More recently, the idea has been given a new impetus and a new definition by Rolf Potts in *Vagabonding*, in which the term is simply defined as "a deliberate way of living that makes freedom to travel possible" (having in mind long-term travel). In this book, the term is used as synonymous to "traveling for traveling's sake."

Tibetan nomads. Amdo, Tibet, Western China.

The world-traveler must, on the one hand, be ready (and actually seek) to visit a tribe in the Solomon Islands or stay with Tibetan nomads; on the other hand, he has to be prepared, when it is required, to wear his suit to attend a classical music concert in a big metropolis. Just as an important part of exploring Brazil is to visit its shantytowns, it is an important part of understanding the French culture to eat at a gourmet restaurant in Paris. It is not *necessary* that the traveler experiences the expensive side of Paris, but he should not reject it because it is outside his own familiar world, or because of the cost. He should account for it in his budget, and plan to attend at least one such event to get a glimpse into a whole new world of Parisian life that is not immediately visible and cannot be experienced in any other way. Similarly, the traveler must not shrink back from those parts of a culture that make him feel uneasy. He must not avoid geographical regions because they seem too cold or too hot, or shy away from cramped minibuses because they are uncomfortable. [Chickens]

Only by adopting an all-encompassing approach and embracing what is central in each region and culture can one truly experience the real world in all its aspects. A backpacker who eschews high culture, identifying with a "style" of travel that ought to be low-cost, will miss as much as a luxury traveler who sees the main sites of a city from the comfort of a modern luxury bus, without ever understanding anything about the everyday life of the locals.

One might say that the "Middle Way" of travel is the best: neither too much luxury and comfort, nor excessive preoccupation with money and roughing it. As a general philosophy of both travel and life, the "all in good measure" of the ancient Greeks and Buddhists is something of an ideal aspiration. Still, it is not just a matter of striking a right balance between the modes of travel (expensive versus economical, or simple versus sophisticated). It is a matter of being able to move with equal ease in disparate social environments within the societies themselves. Ideally, the traveler should be able to move within these societies more freely than the citizens of these societies move within their own strata. Carl Jung offered the following advice to his fellow psychologists a century ago, and we might say that something of this sort of all-encompassing attitude ought to be the mantra of a world-traveler too:

> The researcher ought to hang up exact science and put away the scholar's gown, to say farewell to his study, and wander with human heart through the world, through the horror of prisons, madhouses, and hospitals, through drab suburban pubs, in brothels, and gambling dens, through the salons of elegant society, the stock exchanges, the socialist meetings, the churches, the revivals and ecstasies of the sects, to experience love, hate, and passion in every form in one's body.

Short- and Long-Term Travel

Apart from the division of travel into four categories, we may also divide it into two – the first two (one- and two-dimensional travel) will go under the heading of short-term travel, and the remaining (three- and four-dimensional travel) under long-term travel. There is a quantum jump between the second and third types. At first glance, it might be tempting to think that the crucial element that distinguishes short- from long-term travel is the wealth of experience—the fact that extended and richer experiences carry more weight than short and superficial ones. Important though this element is, it does not suffice to explain the crucial difference between the two forms of travel. Another important characteristic of long-term travel is the distance the traveler acquires with respect to the world he is leaving behind. This has two facets: the first is the obvious distance measured in kilometers (away from home). However, the most important facet is the distance measured by Time. It is to this element of Time (with a capital T) that we must now turn, in order to understand and explain the difference between short- and long-term travel.

Time as the Yeast of the Fermentation of Experience

Time is not only an important element in travel. Just as the existential philosophers of the twentieth century would claim, Time is more important to man's condition than space and is actually just as much a constituent element of reality. It is the fourth dimension of Einstein's space-time continuum that constitutes the physical universe; it is the measure of all human events, of evolution, of history; it is the permanent background of everything we do.

Another important function of Time, however, is that it acts as the yeast of the fermentation of experience. Humans are not moths, which have a lifespan of a few weeks or months. We live to be up to 90 or 100 years of age. Our lifespan is connected with the way we grow up embedded in time. It takes time (a full 16 to 18 years) for us to become adults and, as a rule, more than half a century to reach our full potential. Being the species we are, we need time to learn and understand anything.

How are all these ideas related to travel? Short-term travel is not in harmony with our "mode of being in Time." The speed with which short-term travel overwhelms our senses does not allow us to absorb the new elements that enter our life. The necessary fermentation of experience that only Time can enable is lacking, so our contacts with the world remain in unassimilated pieces that never reach the core of our being.

It is only when travel becomes long-term that Time (in its function as the yeast of fermentation) enters the picture. It is only when the longer timeframe harmonizes with the human mode of being in Time that the travel experiences begin to affect the traveler to the core. This transformative element of Time is the crucial quality that distinguishes short- from long-term travel and gives the latter its added transformational dimension.

Integration

As travelers exploring foreign lands, we carry our unconscious prejudices and pre-conceived notions of countries and people. Similarly, the way we view ourselves is based on equally unconscious models of understanding the world (weltaschaung) that were created during our formative years. The new multifaceted experiences we strive to assimilate do not easily fit in our preformed mental boxes of under-standing. We mentally work nonstop to make sense of the new by relating it to and making it "fit into" the old. Sometimes, the new travel experiences shock our being and cannot easily be harmonized with what we already know—or think we know.

We may apply the analogy of the human digestive process to shed light on the way the experiences of long-term travel affect and transform us through an ongo-ing and prolonged fermentation. While we explore, our senses become immersed in another world, constantly ingesting new experiences, just as we ingest food when we eat. We then digest all these diverse experiences, absorb them, and make them our own. Finally, we transmute the new elements and make them part of who we are —they become indistinguishable from our own body. Assimilation is apparently the last stage in the process. However, this is where the digestive system analogy ends.

There is still one more final, yet less obvious stage, which is also the most en-ergy-consuming: *integration*. It may be defined as follows: *Integration is the har-monious marriage of the old with the new*. No assimilated experience can ever truly become our own unless it is related and harmonized with the whole of our past. It is through this final and most transformative stage of a traveler's interaction with the world—the culmination of the fermentation by Time—that the new will mod-ify the old, so that a new and deeper understanding of the world and one's self may emerge. The degree of success of this integrative function is the measure of the extent to which our travel experiences become one with the totality of our life.

Realizations of the World-Traveler

As the long-term traveler moves further and further along his planned timeline and creates more distance in time from his ordinary life, the new life begins to as-sert itself. His old world begins to fade away both physically and psychologically. He feels free to roam the world without constraints of culture, upbringing, or edu-cation. We may liken this to cutting the umbilical cord that ties the traveler to his own country and culture.

As the journey extends in time, several transformative realizations occur that are accompanied by a deepening of understanding and a new way of feeling and seeing. The traveler begins to experience both his relationship with the world and with his journey and life in a new way. Although many realizations occur during a long-term journey, there are a few that are almost certain to arise and become

The lush, green, cultivated fields contrast with the barren Himalayan mountaintops. A typical summer landscape in Tibetan Buddhist Ladakh, India.

central for the long-term traveler. These realizations are indicative of what happens to the traveler over a long period, and also show the transformative role of time. The order in which they occur depends on the particulars of each journey and the character, age, and background of each traveler.[11] We will examine six of these central realizations in more detail.

The World Is Huge

The world is huge! This is one of the first and most shocking realizations of a world-traveler. It is truly surprising how much bigger it is than most of us think. We all grow up measuring distances with the ruler and units of our own country. For Europeans, who live in the second-smallest continent of the planet and use as their measuring rod distances from Frankfurt to Paris and Rome to Vienna, the sizes of most non-European countries turn out to be much bigger than they could ever have imagined. But even Americans or Chinese, who might not be so impressed by the sizes of other countries, soon discover that their own seemingly huge countries are but a very small part of a much grander whole.

Very few people realize that Mexico is more than five times the size of Germany. Or that Brazil is the size of the whole of Europe (minus Greenland and Eu-

---

11 These realizations are based on the author's own experiences. While they may not be universal or exhaustive of the range of other possible realizations, they probably would be experienced to some degree by most world-travelers. They are presented roughly in the order in which they occurred during the author's journey.

Gelug Monks, the Yellow Hat Sect, chanting before entering the temple at Labrang Monastery. Amdo, Tibet, Western China.

ropean Russia). Japan, being next to immense China, seems to be the size of England, yet in fact it is larger than Germany. And the inconspicuous, almost invisible Antarctica is actually half the size of Africa!

People forget that the maps we use are two-dimensional, artificial portrayals of a sphere, and that almost everything in them is distorted. There is no substitute for studying an actual three-dimensional globe in order to understand, and more importantly feel, the size of the Earth and the interrelationship of its landmasses and oceans. When one carefully studies the three-dimensional globe, one immediately discovers how small Europe is (only two percent of the total surface area of the Earth), and also how far north it is situated. One also realizes that Africa is actually much bigger in size than it appears to be on a two-dimensional map and that Australia is in fact smaller than Brazil. Another shocking observation when examining the globe up close is that the landmasses of the Earth (the main objects of exploration of a world-traveler) comprise less than one-third of its total surface.

The World Is Providing

> *Snow lions don't freeze in snow mountains*
> *Vultures don't fall out of the sky*
> *Fish don't drown in water*
> *Practitioners don't die of hunger.*
> *So cast away this life's concerns!*
> *Give up plans for the future!*
> — Shabkar[12]

The monks enter the temple and leave their boots behind.

Every living organism exists by virtue of its being adapted to its environment. Every organism is provided by Nature with everything it needs for its survival, growth, and reproduction. Since a human being is an organism too, then every human being is similarly being taken care of. Just as a wolf searches and finds its deer, and as a bird finds its seeds, every human finds what his body and mind search for. What Shabkar's poem says in the simplest words is that any fear of dying, any fear of not being provided for, is unfounded. Any such fear is actually contradicted by the most obvious facts of life if we but observe them in their utter simplicity.

Yet, out of fear of the unknown, a large part of the world's population never travels. At its heart is the fear that one's needs will not be taken care of, that one will wander alone and helpless in the world. That is why the majority of those who travel choose to do so in a manner that allows them to feel as though they have never left their comfort zones. The majority of travelers who choose to join group tours do so not just to save money but also to feel safe and secure and to have the certainty that nothing will go wrong. Behind modern mass tourism lies an unexpressed fear of the unknown.

A second fear is that of not being in control. The modern travel agency or tour operator solves both: It makes the unknown seem known by showing photos of the places to be visited, and it deals with the fear of the traveler not being in control by offering its own control over the way one will travel—it provides fixed itineraries and detailed schedules. The traveler therefore buys the illusion of both

---

12 Shabkar Tsokdruk Rangdrol (1781-1851) was a wandering Tibetan Buddhist hermit and poet. In this poem, he addresses aspiring hermits who in Tibet often lived alone in remote retreats.

The Stone

New York City, USA

SECOND DAY in New York City. As I walk along Madison Avenue, I notice that the zipper of my jacket is broken and I can't pull it up. Being an experienced zip-fixer, I see that I need to take off my jacket and find a heavy object in order to hit the pull-tab to straighten it. I start searching for a medium-sized stone. I search in a nearby planter, I look under a tree trunk, I approach a small island of grass – nothing. I can't find a stone. I search along the line where the road meets the sidewalk, I search around a small construction site – to no avail. I cannot find a single stone in New York!

Stone: the symbol of the beginning of civilization, the main material of the Earth's crust on which we all stand. Yet, here I am, surrounded by asphalt, concrete, metal structures, and impressive skyscrapers that touch the clouds, and I cannot find a single stone. At the same time, I see thousands of crafted stones – be it marble or granite – adorning the facades of many buildings. But all these stones are trapped, immobile. What I need is a simple *free stone!*

What an irony: The first thing I happen to search for in New York is the *only* thing it does not have. This incredible metropolis has everything you can possibly think of, yet it lacks the most ubiquitous object in nature – and the only tool that can repair my zipper.

What is great about Shabkar's poem is that it takes the fear of the unknown to its extreme and identifies it with the fear of dying. What is the worst thing the unknown can do to you? Kill you! If the worst of all fears is dealt with by observing that "fish don't drown in water," then by realizing the universality of this principle of Life, all other lesser fears ought to vanish. If the fear of dying is removed, what is there to fear? Shabkar's poem also implicitly deals with the fear of losing control. It says that Nature is permanently in control of everything within its domain, which is *everything*. One is never actually in control. Nature is. And Nature is always providing. We may actually identify Nature with the universe itself, and even come to see its power of sustenance as being none other than the Divine Providence of religions. This Providence is not something remote or ethereal in the sky. It is actually palpable and constantly envelops our whole being. Everything that sustains us is part of this Providence, be it the air we breathe or the food we eat.

What is less easily acknowledged is the highest expression of this Providence: our fellow human beings. As social beings, we grow up in a society and are constantly sustained by a human community. The overwhelming majority of our fellow humans are more than willing to help us when we are seen to need help or when we explicitly ask for it. "Practitioners don't die of hunger," not only because Nature provides for plenty of food and shelter, but also because other practitioners will visit the hermit in his hermitage and bring him whatever he needs. Similarly, all the needs of a traveler are met through his interactions and dealings with other humans. Whatever he needs is always there to meet him. There is food and shelter,

Peligroso!

Valparaiso, Chile

I WAS HAVING A NICE, relaxing, self-indulgent stroll in the streets of Valparaiso, taking much pleasure in observing the people returning home from work, the changing colors of the city as it moved from day to night, the little cobbled streets, the smells, the sounds. In a leisurely manner, I was in complete harmony with the spirit of the city, feeling good with myself and my surroundings.

At some moment, I casually asked a passerby for directions to Parque Italia. He stopped, looked at me terrified, became stiff and serious, and exclaimed: "There are bandits and thieves there. You must not go! *Peligroso!* (Dangerous!)" Baffled by this exaggerated claim, I replied, "It's only 7:00 pm – how can it be dangerous!?" Around me I could see hundreds of people filling the streets in the midst of the early evening rush hour. There was nothing ominous in the air. The only person who seemed to be in any panic was the passerby who kept repeating *"Peligroso! Peligroso!"* as our ways parted.

Instinctively, and trying to recover from the sudden little shock he gave me, I headed towards a main road parallel to the cobbled street I was already walking on. I then immediately caught myself thinking about petty thieves and gangs who might attack me, and about the fact that I might unwittingly, in spite of all indications to the contrary, really be walking in a dangerous city. Suddenly, all the beautiful little things I was observing and enjoying started to lose their romantic and picturesque character. They became tainted by an element of doubt. I wondered, "Is it possible that this interesting historic city is dangerous? Am I a stupid visitor strolling around unaware of all the dangers that surround me?" But how could I erase what I saw – a normal city going about its normal life?

These thoughts didn't last for long, for I had already decided to follow the suggested walk of my tourist map that included Parque Italia. After a couple of minutes, I reached Parque Italia. What did I see? High school kids! They were gathering near bus stops to return home or sitting on the many benches in the nice plaza, embracing and kissing one another or telling jokes and having fun. Amidst the high school students there were other people heading home from work. Not an inkling of danger, not a hint of anything being wrong. How funny, I thought, that of all the places I had visited that day, Parque Italia – the only one the passerby had warned me about – turned out to be the safest of all, the least dangerous, filled with the sights and sounds of high school kids enjoying their youth.

Bandits are not hiding at every corner waiting for the right moment to attack us. The overwhelming majority of mankind consists of normal people going about their daily lives and routines. Bandits constitute an infinitesimal minority in our world, and they usually act in stealth and do minimal harm. The real bandits are inside our heads – it is *they* who cause the gravest harm.

means of travel and information, a computer to connect with the world, and above all, other people to ask for advice or help.

After a few months of travel, every long-term traveler begins to experience this self-evident and ever-present reality of a *providing world* – which is a more limited, practical, and nonreligious expression of the more all-encompassing concept of Divine Providence. After a year or so, this becomes a reality that guides one's thoughts and actions. The traveler ceases to over-plan, worry, or have any doubts about the ability to handle whatever problem appears along the way. Even if, at times, the providing world may seem to temporarily fail us for the little needs we never tire of artificially creating [The Stone], Shabkar's absolute certainty that all major problems are solved while an organism is still alive becomes one's governing philosophy. There is a certainty in the traveler's mind that every single thing shall be taken care of as it appears, one by one, day after day.

The World Is Safe

Another central realization that is somehow related to the above, yet is quite distinct, concerns the safety of travel. Most travel books are obsessed with "Annoyances & Dangers." Sometimes one gets the feeling that these travel-guide writers believe that they move in a hostile and dangerous world. Reading these chapters, the traveler may subsequently become obsessed with matters of security and safety.

During the early parts of a journey, the traveler may be a bit conscious of security and safety and heed the books' warnings by being cautious at night and avoiding certain areas. Yet, as one moves through the world and obtains a more complete picture of the nature of other societies and cultures, one begins to understand that the exact opposite is true: *The world is an amazingly safe place.*

The real outside world is no different than the world each one of us happens to be in right now—do you see any danger around you, do you feel unsafe right now? Notwithstanding extremely rare and special cases, the world is as safe as it is around you as you read this book. Being run over by a car is more probable than being violently robbed or attacked in the street, yet we go on crossing streets. The rule is what matters, not the exception. It is such a pity that so many people base their decisions and even their whole lives on the rare exceptions of life.

This simple truth is disguised by myths that people create and then believe. These are myths about criminals, dangers, "bad neighborhoods," or countries and even continents to avoid. Those who believe in these myths have often never left their own countries. Some do not even dare to walk a few blocks from their own houses for fear of criminals. However, those fears exist only in the mind, in the imaginary worlds that people create, replacing the real world they never get to know. [Peligroso!]

We live not only in a safe world, but also in a *friendly* world. Wherever we go, we are surrounded by helpful people who treat us with kindness and respect. Everywhere, there are swarms of people who come to assist us—whether we are engaged in the trivial search for a toilet or the more complicated task of finding the right hotel. The overwhelming majority of people are kind, helpful, openhearted,

*Muslim university
students having
a break.
Ternate, Indonesia.*

polite. A surprisingly huge number even go to extremes to assist the traveler. Many people may go out of their way to walk you to a junction so that they are sure you do not get lost, others go about trying to solve a problem you have as if it is their own, while others invite you into their home or to their son's wedding.

Another myth is that the off-the-beaten-track destinations are more difficult or more dangerous than the well-known ones. This could not be further from the truth. In more touristy destinations, which have professional services for the traveler's needs, people tend to take the traveler for granted and be less helpful. Of course, all the comforts provided by the tourist industry itself—which is, as a rule, helpful and friendly—more than make up for this tendency of people accustomed to tourists to be less helpful. However, in the less-touristy destinations, where comforts are less and know-how scarce, the average man on the street enters into the picture to make up for the deficiency. Every person in a small and isolated village offers to become your guide, your helper, or your guardian angel.[13]

Universal Belonging

Humans need to belong. From the moment we are born, we belong to our family, our clan, our nation. We grow up belonging to classrooms, sports teams, fraternities, religious or civic associations. Many people even obtain their sense of iden-

---

13 One thing I always found amusing is that sometimes people whom I had just met would accompany me at night in a supposedly "infamous neighborhood" in order to protect me. However, since I hardly knew them, they had an equal chance of belonging to the group of people they were protecting me from!

tity through such identifications and memberships. Some feel that belonging to a group excludes others, and often those excluded form the entity with respect to which the group obtains its own feeling of self-identity. "Us" versus "the others" is often part and parcel of the idea of this type of belonging. Yet true belonging becomes perverted through such limited views.

One of the first experiences of a world-traveler is the realization that he need not make any special effort to belong. He neither gives belonging any special attention, nor does he strive for it. This is a liberating feeling. We may call it "freedom from the idea of belonging." One becomes liberated from the conditioned and unconscious craving for belonging to a group in order to feel "normal." The traveler learns to accept his aloneness as natural and proper, while effortlessly relating to others. He then comes to feel comfortable in his aloneness and realizes that it is neither loneliness nor isolation. As we will see in Chapter III, it is actually identical to solitude—a solitude amidst the world. Living in solitude means affirming our separateness and uniqueness as something natural, proper, and good. It also means affirming that there is no need to belong to any group, for we already belong to humanity as a whole, while maintaining our individual character.

The realization that one need not belong in order to *truly* belong creates a new awareness of belonging to the world. This sense of belonging naturally expands to include all of humanity in its infinite variety and modes of expression. We may call this the realization of *universal belonging*. There is a new sense of freedom associated with this. It is not a feeling that one is free *from* society, since one is moving through many societies. It is rather a freedom *within* society. It is the freedom to be one's true self, disregarding the common criteria of what one ought to be in order to belong to a social group or to society as a whole. One already belongs to society by default, by virtue of being human, irrespective of how one leads one's life. True belonging, unlike the false sense of belonging that results from superficial and often alienating conformity, is all-inclusive—it accepts all groups and nations in it, but also all individuals. It is only when one faces oneself in solitude and accepts the reality of one's differentiated nature and uniqueness that one begins to see in others the same expression of uniqueness and individuality. One then comes to see society in a new light: not as a medley of random units composing a mass, but as an entity full of potentialities, which is creative to the degree to which its individual elements retain and express their uniqueness in the whole. It is through the affirmation of one's aloneness, individuality, and uniqueness that a consummate realization of true belonging arises.

The Journey Has a Life of Its Own

You think it is *your* journey. Yet there comes a point when you begin to serve it as much as it serves you. You no longer hold the reins. The journey begins to take on

Termite Mound. Wayanad Sanctuary, Kerala, India.

a life of its own. Just as Eugène Marais's[14] theory that the termite colony as a whole is a single organism, and the termites function as the cells of its body, you start to feel like an insignificant termite serving the journey. Or, as Carl Jung[15] liked to say about complexes, you realize that you do not "own" the journey, but rather *it owns you.*

This does not happen suddenly. At first you are the sole master of the journey—or so you think. Then many things begin to happen that are beyond your control. Occasionally, you feel a mysterious impelling drive to be at a place at a specific time, or an urge to open a conversation with a person who has curiously gotten your attention. At other times, little misfortunes seem to resist your plans and your journey. However, you begin to have an inkling that these seemingly unwelcomed occurrences had a purpose. For example, everything you have planned for the day may seem to go wrong, yet by chance you end up staying at a remote lodge whose owner turns out to be the most interesting person you have met in that country! At times you feel as if a place has cast a spell on you and for no ap-

---

14 Eugène Marais (1871-1936), a South African naturalist, proposed this theory in his book *The Soul of the White Ant*. According to Marais, the specialization of each group of termites corresponds to the specialization of the cells of the human body. Thus, the termites that use leaves to oxygenate the air inside the mound are the lungs of the colony, the ones that create a special coating on the exterior surface of the mound to protect it from the rain are the skin, the queen in the heart of the colony that controls everything is the brain, and so on.

15 Carl Gustav Jung (1875-1961), a famous psychotherapist and one of the most influential thinkers of the twentieth century: "Everyone knows nowadays that people 'have complexes.' What is not well known, though far more important theoretically, is that complexes can *have us.*" (*A Review of the Complex Theory*, par. 204.)

parent reason, you cannot depart. Your feet seem to be shackled to the Earth and you *know* you have to extend your stay for a few days. A week later, you happen to stumble across a special ceremony at your next stop. You then realize that you would have missed the ceremony had you not lingered in that other place earlier.

The whole experience is that, in spite of all your itineraries, plans, and efforts, the things you do not control are so numerous, and their cumulative effect so huge, that "your" journey becomes a composite made of both your plans and the unexpected. Surprisingly, you end up realizing that these unexpected and uncontrolled elements are actually the larger part of the journey. You sense that, although you seem to be making the decisions, in truth, another force is in control. There is a feeling of being moved like a marionette by invisible strings. The journey seems to be infused with some kind of vital force; it resembles a living entity with needs of its own, requiring attention and care. From being the supposed master of the journey, you begin to feel like a caretaker. You realize that what you called your journey—a line upon a map, an itinerary upon a calendar, a set of experiences written in a diary—is neither owned by you nor derived from your own plans and actions. Rather, your plans and actions are guided by it; the journey itself is the force, controlling everything you do.

There is a poignant passage in Sri Aurobindo's epic poem *Savitri* that expresses this feeling and idea in remarkable poetic language. The image of "the conscious Doll" that is pushed a hundred ways is a metaphor, not only of our life's-journey, but also of any long-term travel-journey, both of which, as we will see in Chapter IV, are inextricably interrelated. It is worth quoting the passage:

> A thinking puppet is the mind of life:
> Its choice is the work of elemental strengths
> That know not their own birth and end and cause
> And glimpse not the immense intent they serve.
> In this nether life of man drab-hued and dull,
> Yet filled with poignant small ignoble things,
> The conscious Doll is pushed a hundred ways
> And feels the push but not the hands that drive.
> For none can see the masked ironic troupe
> To whom our figure-selves are marionettes,
> Our deeds unwitting movements in their grasp,
> Our passionate strife an entertainment's scene.

At this stage, the traveler begins to harmonize his movements with what the journey itself seems to suggest. He begins to see a particular course of travel, or a particular course of action within the foreign land, as being more or less in self-harmony. Harmony becomes something concrete and recognizable, not an ab-

Defeat

Siladen, Indonesia

"... AND IN THE MIDST of his originally planned four-year journey around the world, the weary Greek traveler arrived in the cluster of 18,000 islands of Indonesia, the heart of which is no other than the notorious Spice Islands, in search of which, five centuries ago, the Great Magellan lost his life in a battle with the natives.

"After having lived through every possible experience and imaginable adventure, our traveler was not afraid of dying. However, as all real or imaginary heroes, he was to be finally subdued by an unforeseen, invisible enemy with power even superior to Death itself. At the exact moment he was about to reveal to the world his great achievement of having managed to follow Magellan's route up to the point where the latter perished; at the exact moment he would have triumphantly proclaimed that he had traversed half the globe in two-and-a-half years, just then, he received a blow even worse than the death blow of his predecessor. For it was better to die than bear the following *realization*; something quite simple that now assumed supernatural proportions and significance:

"He had planned to see the most important parts of the world in four years, and now, after careful study and consideration, he realized that he needed more than four years to explore, or rather scratch the surface, of the most important parts of Indonesia alone! With 1,000 inhabited islands, this seemingly small corner of the planet turned out to be an immense galaxy unto itself. The accumulated enormity of these islands transcends the limits of our globe. Through their apparent smallness, like grains of sand, they stretch out to reach the infinity of the universe. It now became clear to him that our planet, though seemingly finite, is destined to remain forever unknowable and unexplorable. For even if all else is known and traversed, there will always remain the Infinite Microcosm of Indonesia — the fatal battleground of any world-traveler.

"The exhausted Greek traveler folded his maps, closed his books, and accepted, like all heroes do, including the honorable Magellan, who stood at that exact place before him, his final irreversible capitulation. He had nothing to proclaim to the world but this tragic and dishonorable defeat — one with no battle, no clashing of swords, no clamor and blood. A defeat brought about by this, unknown to anyone but him, silent realization. 'Silent as dots on a disk of snow.'"*

* The final line of the poem "Safe in their Alabaster Chambers" by Emily Dickinson (1830-1886).

straction. The degree to which one learns to listen to the voice of the journey is the degree to which one enjoys the journey and benefits from it. This experience of self-harmony is actually identical to the uncontrived, free-flowing mode of travel that becomes predominant after this stage.

Of course, harmony is often lost and regained throughout the journey. Whether this harmony is present or not at any particular moment is not as important as the realization and feeling that it actually exists as a permanent reality in his movement in the world. It is this constant inner awareness of the presence

A modest Hindu ceremony: Scattering the ashes of a deceased loved one into the sea. Bali, Indonesia.

of travel-harmony that enables the long-term traveler to bear all difficulties and persevere in his endeavor.

The World Is Unknowable

The final and most important realization of all comes after more than a couple of years of traveling. It both shocks and overpowers the traveler's psyche: He realizes that the world is infinite in relation to the finite capabilities of a single human being. This, coupled with a cumulative fatigue, which is the result of both a physical and psychological overstretch after years on the move, makes the traveler understand that his journey can never accomplish its original target. There is no way a world-traveler may ever actually know the world completely. The world in its totality remains forever a mystery—it can never be entirely captured, but only approached. The most a traveler can accomplish is to form one out of innumerable possible personal outlooks of the world, to create one out of many potential mental maps of it. For when all the experiences are merged—landscapes, peoples, happenings—each and every traveler becomes a unique vessel into which the world is poured in order for a single subjective vision to be formed. Every traveler sees his own world colored by his own subjectivity, and no two conceptions of the world will ever coincide. This unique synthesis that each traveler creates is his own "personal portrait" of the Earth, never before constructed and never to be repeated. In this sense, the traveler's experience of the world is like a work of art. And although it is subjective, it carries within it objective *truth* and *value* like all works of art carry. It is thus easier for the traveler to live with the realization of the impossibil-

*Preparing
for a big Hindu
festival.
Bali, Indonesia.*

ity of actually knowing the world by positioning his endeavor in the sphere of art
and seeing himself as an artist!

What is more disturbing, though, is the realization that it is not even *physically* possible to "see the world." We can accept that we can never know or come to a
common objective understanding of the world as a whole. But we always feel that
when it comes to the physical world, it may seem possible, within the confines of
a finite journey lasting for a few years or a lifetime, to see the whole of our planet.
We think that the world is comprised of a finite number of attractions, peoples,
and cultures. However, after more than a couple of years of traveling—probably
earlier if the traveler is more discerning—there comes the realization that even
this is not possible. The world-traveler cannot physically see the whole world, irrespective of how many years he spends traveling.

This is so because, as it turns out, within the finite borders of our planet there
exist myriad "infinite microcosms": unique places with an incredible density of
natural and cultural content. An example of a *geographical* infinite microcosm is
the thousands of islands of Indonesia. It takes decades to simply visit all of them,
probably many lives to truly explore them. We may call this the "Indonesian realization." Whether it is connected with the real Indonesia or not, it comes to shake
the foundations of the world-journey itself. **[Defeat]**

But the infinity inherent in the world's cultures is just as daunting. The innumerable traditions of the Balinese culture, for example, are a *cultural* infinite microcosm. Irrespective of how long you explore the traditions, rituals, arts and crafts,
music, religion, and more of this small island, you will always feel there is more to
explore. Yet the commonest infinite microcosms are actually the ones nearer to us:

Young Buddhist monks in Mon Village outside Yangoon, Myanmar.

our own cities! We are unaware of this because we are constantly immersed in them. London, for example, with its approximately 200 museums, over 800 attractions of all types, thousands of restaurants and clubs—and a ceaselessly renewed stream of theater plays, concerts, and events—is an *urban* infinite microcosm. The more you explore it, the more you discover that you can never truly know it. Another such urban microcosm, of a totally different character, is medieval Fez in Morocco. Fez contains history and treasures of never-ending diversity. Both London and Fez are microcosms because they are contained in a small area of the Earth, but they are also infinite because their substance is spread over many other dimensions beyond the physical. A city is not just its monuments, parks, and buildings, but also its history, art, society, and cultural life. Along each alleyway of historic Fez and behind each door of central London, there are myriad hidden worlds to be discovered, layers to be uncovered. Likewise, most great metropolises of the world are so inexhaustible that they are forever being explored even by their own permanent residents!

The awareness of the impossibility of one's arbitrary little track to capture the totality of the world becomes the catalyst for another important related realization: *One may choose to end one's journey at any single moment.* Coming to terms with the futility of trying to "see the world," there is no more "need" to travel. What then keeps the traveler traveling is not some purpose to be achieved or some work to be accomplished but the wonderment at the infinity of the world. After this crucial point, the engine that drives the wheel of travel becomes none other than one's need to come to terms with this unknowable infinity, all the while postponing the journey's end in order to experience more of the world's ceaseless stream of wonders and surprise.

* * *

We have seen that our whole planet may be viewed as one single Destination Earth and that world travel is not only possible, but it will most probably become one of the defining human activities of this century. We also explained that long-term world travel is in harmony with our human mode of "being in Time," and we discussed some of the most potent realizations that are almost certain to come about in any world-journey.

The moment has come to investigate the ideas that will form the foundation upon which any future world travel will be based. We first need to create some new concepts and introduce a new vocabulary within which world travel may be viewed and discussed. Then, we need to examine the mindset of the new world-traveler—the attitude and general principles that will guide his travels. But we also need to describe his actual mode of being while he is on the move, and finally relate it to the whole of life. In the next chapter, we will be exploring this nascent field, which we may rather ambitiously call "a new philosophy of travel."

CHAPTER III
A NEW PHILOSOPHY OF TRAVEL

The twentieth century witnessed an onslaught of new niche philosophies about practically everything, from the philosophy of biology to the philosophy of language. Yet there has not been any elaborate philosophical or even abstract discussion about travel. This chapter aims to fill the gap, not by creating a formal system of yet another theoretical or academic philosophy, but by introducing and discussing practical concepts that pertain to the praxis of travel. As travel becomes more common, it is time to shed some fresh light upon it in order to help the billions of present and future travelers to place their travels and explorations into a framework that will assist them in making wise decisions.

What follows is a simple approach to travel, which is the result of the fusion of actual travel experiences with ordinary common sense. The ideas are divided into three sections. In the first section, some new concepts related to the exploration of a country are introduced. In the second section, many of the elements that constitute the mindset for long-term and world travel are described and examined thoroughly. Finally, we explore the travel mode of being.

A. NEW CONCEPTS RELATED TO THE EXPLORATION OF A COUNTRY

Three new concepts pertaining to long-term travel are introduced. The first one deals with the depth of our exploration of a country, the second with how we choose the field of our exploration and how we go about moving within a country, and the third deals with the final aim of travel.

Magnification

When examining a living cell under a microscope, we use lenses of various magnifications to see different aspects of it. The lens magnification (say 50× or 1000×) determines the level of detail we see. With this analogy in mind, let us introduce a new concept in travel: *magnification.* Magnification is the measure of depth with which one explores a country or region. It lies at the heart of planning, and it secretly guides the way one travels, the speed of travel, and the mode of exploration. It is obvious that the depth with which one explores a country depends primarily on the time one has available—the length of the journey. Clearly, a three-week visit to Australia is of a much lower magnification than a three-month journey. What the first traveler will experience and understand in three weeks will pale in comparison to that of the latter.

Though it might not be obvious, there is no actual limit to the depth of exploration. The more time one spends exploring a country—the more regions he sees, the longer he stays in each region, and the more he studies—the deeper his exploration will be. Let us not forget, for example, that there are social anthropologists who have spent their entire careers studying one single tribe of the South Pacific without having exhausted what there is to learn about it! A country like China, with a five-thousand-year continuous history, many indigenous peoples, and a great variation of local customs, will always have something new and deeper to reveal to us with each increasing magnification of exploration.

We may be certain that a low magnification of exploration will not give us access to the heart and soul of a country and its cultures. If one simply wants to get a very superficial taste of a country—a perfectly legitimate quest—then one may decide to travel, say, around Australia for three weeks and gather glimpses from this continent in meze-like fashion. At the end of such a low-magnification exploration, he will not be said to have "seen" Australia, nor have related with its heart and soul. His exploration, being superficial and brief, will have been akin to leafing through a book in order to know what it is about without actually reading it. On the other end of the spectrum, there is no limit to how high magnification may go. If one lives in China for 20 years, he will definitely come to understand the country and culture much better than any passing traveler can ever do. Yet there must be some law of diminishing returns that appears somewhere along this seemingly infinite line of increasing magnification. The person living in China for 20 years will not learn twice as much about China during the second decade of his residence. We will not be wrong in assuming that after 10 years of living there, provided that he has immersed himself wholeheartedly in the Chinese culture, he may even be said to have *become* Chinese. There will be no significant aspects of that culture unknown to him—though there will always be an infinite number of books he may read to further deepen his understanding, and hundreds more parts of China to visit.

But how does a serious traveler approach the subject of magnification? There is no correct magnification for exploring any country. This is always related to the fixed time limits the traveler may impose on his journey. He may thus proceed in two ways: He may decide beforehand how much time he has for traveling and then choose the magnification of his exploration accordingly, or he may decide in advance the magnification and make the length of travel conform to it.

The world-traveler must naturally belong to the second category: He decides on the depth of exploration first (the magnification) and then adapts the length of travel accordingly. But how does he decide on the magnification with which he will explore a country if there is no upper limit to it? Shouldn't there be some *guiding principle* that would help decide the measure of depth of any exploration?

Meditating on the subject, it becomes obvious that there are three important elements that determine the mode of a traveler's exploration. One is objective; the other two are subjective. The objective element relates to the hard facts and realities of a country, such as its size, the wealth of its natural landscapes, the depth of its culture and history. The second element has to do with each traveler's personal interests, while the third relates to the final object of the traveler's endeavor.

From the objective standpoint, whereas both the United States and Cyprus are equally sovereign countries, the United States consists of 50 states, 48 of which happen to be larger than Cyprus. Each U.S. state may be considered, for the sake of travel, as a separate country. The United States, therefore, is actually akin to a whole continent like Europe, when its size, wealth of natural landscapes, and regional diversity are taken into account. Even if Cyprus has a much longer recorded history, going back a few thousand years, still, to explore the little island, a few days to a couple of weeks would be sufficient. The United States is huge by all measures, and many months are necessary to come to grips with both its size and its incredible natural wealth and regional diversity. One must always begin by taking into account these objective and unalterable realities of every place.

Yet these alone are not sufficient to help one decide the magnification with

A carpet of a billion pink daisies of the Siberian prairie in spring. Russia.

which to explore a country. One's personal interests also must be taken into account. These interests are inseparable from what we value in life in general and from the way we see the world. A professor of Byzantine art might decide that *his* proper magnification for exploring Cyprus should be at least a month, for he might intend to delve much deeper into Cyprus's rich world of Byzantine art. He might also decide to visit most of the island's historical sites and museums, and even stay for a week in a Christian Orthodox monastery that has kept alive many Byzantine traditions. His Cyprus turns out to be a much more important place than many other destinations. Similarly, for a mountaineer or trekker, the United States or Nepal cannot be properly explored unless he spends extra time trekking in different parts of those countries and climbing some of their most challenging mountains. It is the harmonious blending of the *objective elements* of a country with the *subjective interests* and worldview of the traveler that in the end determines the magnification with which to explore the regions of a country.

The third and final element relates to the overall aim of the traveler: What is the endeavor of a long-term traveler? Before we tackle this, we need to introduce another concept.

The Wise-Line

The surface of the Earth, even though it is curved, may be considered two-dimensional. But when we travel, we are moving along a line, a one-dimensional path. Therefore, we can never actually, truly explore a surface. So how does a traveler explore the Earth? The only way to actually "fill in" a surface with a line is by a

*Flower fields
with manicured
rolling hills in the
background.
Biei, Hokkaido,
Japan.*

zigzag motion, similar to the one by which children shade a square or a circle by repeatedly moving their pencil from left to right. This kind of motion is not an option for a traveler. It would also be unwise because many adjacent regions of the Earth are similar and one would simply go over these similar areas many times.

Since we are condemned by natural law to simply travel along a line, we might as well turn this line into a "wise" one. We can make it cut through the country's most characteristic landscapes, villages, towns, and cultures in such a way that the line will become a representative *cross section* of the country. Through study and planning, we may identify these points or regions of interest and then draw the best connecting thread between them, creating a wise travel-route. This travel-route becomes, in effect, a wise cross section that aims to capture, with the least possible waste of energy and backtracking, the elements of the country that are most representative of the whole. We may call this representative cross section of exploration of a country the *wise-line.*

But how do we go about drawing this wise-line? The first element that determines its shape, and more importantly, its length, is the magnification with which we have already decided to explore the country. However, to decide upon the correct magnification we must also deal with a second important element: *isolating the common characteristics* of the country. Each country is composed of different geographical, cultural, and architectural regions. Each of these regions is characterized by common elements that are usually found over an extended area. So, when we speak of the bayous of Louisiana in the United States, or the endless expanse of Siberia in Russia, or the beautiful flower fields of Hokkaido in Japan, we refer to huge regions that are defined by common geographical traits and

The Chan Chan ruins, the largest pre-Columbian adobe city in South America. Santa Catalina, Peru.

features. One need not explore all the bayous of Louisiana, or traverse the whole length and width of Siberia or Hokkaido in order to see these regions. The exploration of a small representative part is sufficient to give the traveler a good idea of the whole—just as tasting a mouthful of wine is sufficient for a sommelier to evaluate it.[16]

If we take Peru as an example, we will immediately see that it is composed of three main geographical zones: the coastal desert, the Andes mountain range, and the Amazon rainforest. One need only explore a part of the Amazon in order to experience "Amazonian Peru," and only a part of the coastal desert to see that part of the country. Within this coastal desert strip, several Amerindian civilizations have flourished. Just as with the geographical zones, one need not visit all of the sites of these civilizations in order to obtain an understanding of their character and achievements. It is sufficient to visit only some of the most characteristic or famous ones, such as the adobe city of Chan Chan. Drawing a wise-line connecting these well-selected, representative ancient ruins, as well as adding a trip (or even an adventure) to the actual desert itself, is sufficient to get to know the Peruvian coastal strip—both culturally and geographically.

Of course, the wise-line ought to include not just specific geographical and cultural/historical sites but also parts of the living culture of a country as it is expressed through the traditions and everyday life of its inhabitants. So the traveler ought to include in his exploration such things as experiencing the Peruvian cui-

---

16 The practical application of this concept, as well as the process of selecting the countries of a continent, is further developed at the end of the book in Addendum I.

The procession of the Virgin Mary at the "Fiesta de la Virgen del Carmen." Paucartambo, Peru.

sine, a Peruvian wedding, a dance club, or workshops where traditional craftsmen ply their skills. One may also choose to experience a Latino-Inca fiesta that has elements of both the Spanish and Inca cultures. Attending, say, the Fiesta de la Virgen del Carmen in Paucartambo, probably the mother of all Latin American traditional fiestas, is sufficient to get to know what such celebrations look and feel like. An insatiable search for experiencing more of the same runs the risk of turning the journey into a repetitive and exhausting endeavor.

The third element that guides the formation of the wise-line is the honoring of the traveler's special interests, character, and personality. We have already touched upon this when we discussed how magnification is determined by both the country's objective reality and the subjective personal interests of the traveler. In a similar fashion, personal interests play a role in the creation of the wise-line. A traveler who loves adventure in nature may decide to include two days of whitewater rafting in his itinerary. If he loves birds, he may include a bird-watching excursion. If he is a modern history aficionado, he may include a number of World War II sites. The inclusion of many such personal elements is an indispensable part of any itinerary and forms a significant part of the wise-line. Harmonizing the exploration of the country's objective "must-see" aspects with the traveler's personal interests and hobbies is one of the challenges of creating the best possible cross section of a country. The wise-line is *wise* by virtue of it having harmoniously synthesized the objective world with the personal world of the traveler.

It is for this reason that every wise-line is also unique. For the list of personal elements is infinite because there are infinite aspects to life. The list of such elements is infinite, because there are infinite aspects to life. Anything under the sun may be included in one's wise-line if it is meaningful to the traveler. However, significant though the personal aspect is, the long-term traveler must not lose sight of his more important aim to get to know the country itself. He must not easily get carried away with his passions, such as, say, hiking in Nepal, or visiting nightclubs in New York. For he may end up walking along many hills and forests of Nepal, but fail to visit its great temples; or he may come to know how New Yorkers have fun at night, but fail to visit some of the city's great museums. It is quite common to see travelers become totally immersed in their loves or passions, thus experiencing only that small part of a country which goes through the lens of their narrow interests. But a long-term traveler ought to strive for the opposite: to broaden his interests and expand his field of exploration, so that he may discover new things to love and be passionate about! Instead of viewing a country through the limiting lenses of his already established loves and interests, he should allow the country itself to modify, expand, and extend those interests. Only then will he touch the world at new points of which he was previously unaware. Although honoring one's loves, special interests, and individuality is an indispensable part of creating a harmonious wise-line, still, the objective elements of a country ought to be more important in determining the overall course of one's journey.

There is one last element that determines the final *realized* wise-line of exploration. This, however, cannot be planned in advance. It is the joker in the pack of every journey, the mercurial element of life's unpredictability. Let us call it *being open to surprise*—in honor of David Steindl-Rast,[17] who best emphasized its transformative role in our daily life. The traveler plans his route, the places he will visit, the events he will attend, the elements of culture he will focus upon, and so on. However, if travel were only the actualization of preplanned movements, it would end up being like an organized tour. The unique privilege of an independent long-term traveler is his ability to reinvent his journey while he is on the move. He can always change the journey's course, or even abruptly end it and return home! By being in constant relation with Life[18] itself, a traveler has the luxury to adapt his movements to the requirements or the "call" of every moment. By being open to surprise—unexpected encounters, events, abrupt changes in plans—he stays in harmony with the flow of Life.

For example, a traveler may have planned to stay in Uyuni, Bolivia, for a couple of days, but just as he is about to depart he learns that there is a traditional

---

17 David Steindl-Rast (1926-) is a Benedictine monk who has actively participated in interfaith dialogue for the last five decades. His books and lectures inspire individuals worldwide.

18 Here and later on in the chapter, some words are capitalized. This is done to distinguish the all-encompassing abstract meaning of the word from the more limited and ordinary usage of it. Here "Life" means the principle of life, in contrast to "daily life." Later on, "Question" is capitalized to denote "the principle of inquiring"; similarly, "the Becoming" means the process of being transformed, capitalized "Freedom" denotes absolute freedom, and so on.

traders' market in town the next day. He decides to stay longer. In the evening he meets an interesting fellow traveler who recommends that he visit a colorful village in the Salt Desert. So, the next day, he goes to the traders' market, and the day after that, he visits the village.

Most of the surprises are pleasant ones. Yet even the unpleasant ones, such as missing the only bus to the next destination, or getting robbed, or having a stressful interaction with someone, may become opportunities for experiencing new things or discovering unexpected treasures. The extra day of stay due to the missed bus may lead to an encounter with an extraordinary person; reporting the robbery at the police station and experiencing the little nuances associated with it may become the most rewarding day in the country; having a stressful argument with the hotel receptionist may reveal aspects of the local culture that the traveler chose to disregard.

Being open to surprise is almost identical to being open to change. One's planned itinerary is not a holy book. One's plans must always be viewed as tentative. The wise-line cannot be and *never is* wholly preconceived and preplanned. It is alive, just as Life is, and it ends up being wise to the degree to which it conforms to the calls of Life. To become a representative cross section of the country and culture it aims to explore, the wise-line must allow the unpredictable and the surprising to modify it accordingly. It is because of this most important factor of being perpetually flexible that the wise-line has the power to capture the deepest and most valuable elements of a country.

As we saw in the previous chapter, one of the realizations of a world-traveler is that the journey obtains a life of its own and becomes a self-organizing process that constantly adapts itself to its own self-discoveries. Being open to surprise is the most important mechanism through which the journey obtains this "life of its own." And the realized wise-line of the traveler who is always opened to surprise becomes in effect the footprint of this "alive" journey on the surface of the earth.

Having introduced the two concepts of magnification and the wise-line, we are now ready to examine the deeper underlying quest of long-term travel.

Capturing the Soul

The moment has come to relate all of this analysis to an important question we posed earlier: What is the endeavor of a long-term traveler? When he explores a country, what is or ought to be his main aim? Earlier we saw that this is also the third element determining the magnification with which he will decide to explore a country. We also illustrated that this is subjective. This is so because it is impossible to find an objective purpose of travel that would befit all travelers at all times. It is also difficult to suggest to the billions of aspiring travelers the reasons why they may want to travel! Without wanting to diminish all other important endeavors of any traveler—be it marveling at the Earth's inexhaustible wonders; immersing oneself in the rich wealth of archeological, architectural, and other treasures; or even delving into activities such as bird-watching and star-gazing—we have to seek a connecting thread that may give meaning to the totality of one's travel experiences.[19]

There has probably been, throughout the ages, behind every serious travel, a covert, unexpressed, underlying central quest. This quest—sometimes conscious, sometimes unconscious, sometimes appearing as the consummate but unintended outcome of travel—underpins all authentic exploration of any region: the quest to capture its soul. Every region of the world, every country, every place has a soul. This is not easy to define in words because it is inexpressible. However, it is not something that lies outside of our ability to experience, because one may actually know when one has captured it. We may speak of the *capturing of the soul* of a country in terms of a definitive experience.

This experience cannot be planned and cannot be pursued, to borrow an idea from psychiatrist Viktor Frankl,[20] who said, "Happiness cannot be pursued; it must ensue." Similarly, it is not up to the traveler to plan or pursue the capturing of the soul of a country. Firstly, the soul does not exist as an objective entity out there to be captured. Secondly, since the experience of the capturing of the soul does not depend on us, it cannot be willed to happen. Just like Frankl's happiness and meaning, the capturing of the soul may come or it may not, irrespective of the traveler's will or actions. Thirdly, capturing the soul is not the certain mathematical outcome of a set of causes and effects. There is no formula or system whereby one may capture the soul of a country. That said, however, the traveler is not simply at the mercy of fate or circumstances in this regard. Although we cannot force or command this "capturing" to happen at will, there are factors that can facilitate it.

The most important factor that one may be said to control is one's *strength of aspiration*—one's love of travel, will to understand and learn, passion to relate to other cultures. One may aspire to capture the soul of a country by totally immersing oneself into the travel experience. The immersion begins from the moment the journey is conceived, it continues during the period of study and planning, and then throughout the actual travel.

The *mindset* of the traveler is the other important factor, and we will devote the next section to it. Still though, irrespective of the few things in our control—the strength of our aspiration, the meticulous drawing and execution of a wise-line of exploration, and the mindset of the traveler—there is no guarantee of success in this endeavor. The capturing of the soul may come at a specific rec-

---

19 What follows is the exposition of the author's subjective travel endeavor. However, the ensuing analysis aims to establish it as the main universal and objective endeavor of all long-term travel.

20 Viktor E. Frankl (1905-1997), a neurologist and psychiatrist, wrote the classic book *Man's Search for Meaning*, in which he explores the main existential problems of man, including life's meaning and happiness.

ognizable instance, or it may come gradually as the consummation of a process of maturation and deep understanding. Although all the elements that comprise a country—its landscapes, flora and fauna, its natural beauty and wonders—contribute to the formation of its soul, the most important elements are its people and culture. It is this human element that lies at the core of a country's soul. As the traveler delves deeper into the new foreign culture, he comes to feel and know better what it means to be a member of the new culture. If he stays long enough for his relationship with the new culture to reach a certain threshold, then a point might be reached when he truly feels and understands what it is like to be the other: He *becomes*, so to speak, a member of the new culture. He becomes a Bolivian, a Samoan, an Indonesian. It is *this* experience that lies at the heart of what we call the capturing of the soul. **[Kwaio]** Not just observing and studying, but becoming the other is the pinnacle of every real world travel. Even when it comes about as a result of a slow process, there is still a moment when one realizes that one has captured the soul of a culture. From that moment onward, he thinks, feels, and moves within the other culture as if he is an integral member of it. He moves in it effortlessly and with a sense of uncontrived harmony. In some strange fashion, he may feel as if he has *already* been living in this country for years, or as if he could make it his home country and live there for the rest of his life. This feeling of belonging to the country as if it is one's own is not the same as the "home away from home" advertised by tour operators (which is a synonym for carrying one's home comforts into the foreign country). On the contrary, the traveler ends up feeling at home *in spite of* the new country having none of the qualities (or comforts) of his home country. It is a new home: The new country retains all of its elements that were previously alien to the traveler, just as the traveler retains all of the new sensations, feelings, and thoughts that this new country has generated in him. It is a new home because all alienation has vanished.

The moment of capturing the soul is magical. Travel then becomes much more than visiting places and observing other cultures. It becomes something that transforms the core of our being. The "other" becomes internalized and ceases to be an "other" any more. Experiencing what it means to be a member of another society allows you to transcend your national limitations and to supplant your narrow way of seeing the world with a new vision. Then, you realize that having lived your life as a German or an Australian was but an arbitrary spin of the wheel of fate, a mere coincidence of circumstance; that being a member of *any* other culture might have equally been the case. Attachment to one's own culture and grasping onto one's nationality vanishes forever.

Previously, under the discussion of the concept of magnification, we saw that the third element that determines magnification is the endeavor of the traveler. If the traveler truly aims to capture the soul of a country, then the magnification must be very high. The more deeply one is willing to delve into the heart and soul

Kwaio

Malaita, Solomon Islands

"YOU EAT LIKE A KWAIO MAN!" said my guide. "That's what they just said," he added with a triumphant smile.

At that moment, while holding the head of the roasted suckling pig between my hands and immersing my front teeth in the tender flesh of its cheeks, with an entourage of young Kwaio (pronounced: koyo) men staring at me with awe, I knew that my journey in the Solomons had just reached its climax and final fulfillment. I had *become*, if even only for a few seconds, a member of the once fearful Kwaio tribe! I had effortlessly experienced a connection to the tribe's soul, and felt what it was like to be a Kwaio. I had also reconnected with my cannibal roots, something that was at the heart of my quest in this part of the world where cannibalism was once widespread. The fact that the Kwaio did not practice cannibalism, and that the flesh I was devouring was not human, was irrelevant. At that instant, I had come as close as possible to experiencing the sensations of what a cannibal might have felt during a feast.

At the place where the pig was slaughtered and had its intestines cut out, above the stones and leaves of the makeshift earthen pit that was dug in the ground, I saw a group of pigs devouring the leftovers of their roasted comrade without any remorse. They were even picking and eating the cooked leaves upon which some skin or blood happened to have stuck. As it turns out, pigs are, along with thousands of other species, natural cannibals – as our own human species used to be for most of its existence on earth.

I recall the inscription about cannibalism in a display case in the National Museum of Fiji in Suva, which I had found humorous at the time. The immediate ancestors of present-day Fijians were among the last people in the world to practice cannibalism. Embarrassed by this fact, the museum officials attempted to soften their country's cannibalistic history with the following caption: "Cannibalism was an ancient and widespread practice. Research has shown that it occurred all around the world. For example, there was cannibalism in Spain 8,000 years ago, 7,000 in France, 3,000 in Britain and 1,000 years ago in South America and so on. In Fiji, it was as recent as the late 1800s." Apart from the inaccuracies in the caption (for example, the Aztecs were still practicing cannibalism on a grand scale well into the sixteenth century CE), the argument is clear and sound: All humans, and consequently all races, went through this stage during their evolution. This is not to mention the many instances in which, because of food scarcity during war or famine, the practice has often been resumed in modern times as well.

But an important question remains: Nowadays, why won't modern humans eat human flesh *even after* it is dead? A simple and obvious answer might be that we have long since ceased to see ourselves and our fellow humans as pieces of meat. Although made of flesh and bones, we see ourselves as something more than that. We have added many extraneous abstractions onto the flesh – names, personal histories, minds, and souls – and it is no longer what it used to be. That is why we allow the worms to do the dirty job for us.

George Seferis, a contemporary Greek poet, wrote in one of his poems: "we are made of grass." I never quite liked that analogy. It attempts to photosynthesize our animal nature! So, let us make an insolent retort in raw prose: We are made of tender, juicy, warm, tasty flesh. *Edible* flesh, just like the meat of any other animal. It is because of this that we are all can-

Children of the Kwaio tribe playing in the rain. Malaita, Solomon Islands.

nibals *still!* Not because we eat one another (although killing one another is just as bad). We are cannibals because we are *potentially* edible flesh. Apologizing to psychologists and other possible research scientists studying the subject, I have my own strange theory: Our never-ending fascination with the subject of human cannibalism, as well as the lure of stories and movies on the subject, is traceable to our ability *to visualize* our own bodies being consumed by any animal, including another human. In the same way the death of another person disturbs us, in great part because we can project onto him thoughts of our own mortality, the act of cannibalism disturbs us because we can project on the human who is being devoured our own edible flesh. And the reason we can instinctively do this is that deep down, we are still cannibals.

Modern man, by elevating his flesh above the category of edible flesh, has achieved much but also lost a lot. Milton called it *Paradise Lost*; Freud, *Civilization and its Discontents*. Different approaches and descriptions notwithstanding, we are all certain of one thing: There is something permanently missing. The Kwaio never sense such a vacuum. Nor do they have the need to create elaborate religious systems to explain and account for what is missing (they happen to be one of the few remaining tribes without a religion).

Reconnecting to my cannibal roots brought me a step closer to alleviating this default discomfort with our own flesh, which is due to our long and ascending legacy as Homo sapiens. I have certainly not found a lost paradise in the Solomons, and certainly no contented life, as we understand the term. However, I managed to do something just as valuable: I related anew to my raw, flesh-and-bone nature.

of a country, the greater the magnification must be. It is this ultimate quest for the capturing of the soul of the countries and regions of the world that makes every long-term journey last longer than the traveler had originally anticipated.

Capturing the soul of a country may be expanded into a similar quest for capturing the soul of a continent. Although the delineation of continents, just like that of countries, is the result of historical processes and conventions, there are still underlying themes and elements that unite huge parts of the world and set them apart from the rest. Unified Europe, even with its many histories, nations, and languages, has a character and a soul quite distinct from that of Asia or South America. Since the Renaissance, a distinct modern European character has been molded that is felt in Europe's social structures, political institutions, education, and customs. A long-term traveler who has traveled in many European countries will, at some stage, be able to feel the unifying thread that goes through Europe. This yet again indefinable European soul is all-encompassing and includes and expresses the most general aspects of the countries and nationalities that comprise Europe. Similarly, the South American countries pertain to a common Amerindian-Spanish-Portuguese legacy that forms the underlying substratum, which unites the modern South American states even with all their individual differences. Although Asia is much more diverse and cannot easily be said to have a similarly well-identified substratum, there exist large parts of it that have common histories, values, and cultures, such as the countries of the Middle East, or some of the countries of East Asia such as China, Korea, and Vietnam. Therefore, we would be allowed to speak of the soul of the Middle East, or the soul of East Asia.

Finally, at the summit of a world-traveler's quest lies the soul of the Earth, which is discovered through the personal synthesis of each traveler who comes to experience the totality of our planet in his own unique way. Earlier we saw that one of the realizations of a world-traveler is that the world in its entirety is ultimately unknowable. The capturing of our planet's soul is therefore an ongoing endeavor that is never completed. With each new journey and every new addition of a tile in the mosaic of his travel experiences, the traveler reformulates and reshapes his relation with the totality of the Earth and its forever-fleeting soul. Although the Earth includes much more than just human society, humans are the highest expression of life on our planet and are at the center of a traveler's exploration. Experiencing the Earth's soul is therefore irrevocably connected with the traveler's interaction with human cultures and his deepening understanding of human nature. Describing the capturing of the soul of the Earth is beset by the same problems discussed earlier with regards to the capturing of the soul of a country, yet there is one central experience that lies at the center of it and relates to humanity at large: The more the world-traveler explores and knows our planet, the more he comes to feel that he is an integral part of one huge human family. The human qualities and traits he shares with this family are felt to be stronger than all the differences that apparently set him apart from other people. This is examined further in Chapter V.

With these three core concepts—magnification, the wise-line, and capturing the soul—the world-traveler has a framework of concepts with which to approach a country's exploration. Let us now turn to another framework, the long-term traveler's *mindset* of both travel and life.

B. A NEW MINDSET FOR THE WORLD-TRAVELER

There are many elements, attitudes, and ideas that form or ought to form what we may call the mindset of a long-term traveler. In what follows, the most important are examined and explored through the lens of world travel.

Difficulties, Struggles, and the Unpleasant Realities of the World

> *In the unseen providence of things our greatest difficulties are our best*
> *opportunities. A supreme difficulty is Nature's indication to us of*
> *a supreme conquest to be won and an ultimate problem to be solved;*
> *it is not a warning of an inextricable snare to be shunned or of an enemy*
> *too strong for us from whom we must flee.*
> — Sri Aurobindo

> *Surely, it is preferable then to accept the unpleasant, the difficult, the contrary*
> *aspects: for these make any travel experience worthy of the name;*
> *there is always a contradiction between comfort—an objective reached without*
> *sufferance—and the truthful lived experience. The vital component in life,*
> *all that we consider a gain is the fruit of an effort and of a resistance...*
> — Stefan Zweig

As stressed earlier, the *whole* of Life is the field of exploration of the world-traveler. The whole of Life means everything—the difficulties, problems, and pitfalls that are included in the actual act of traveling, plus the disturbing and painful aspects of the world. The world-traveler is completely immersed in the totality of life and thus experiences the total make-up of each place, each society, each circumstance. He is not observing the world from a distance but is totally immersed in it, and therefore sees its "bowels and intestines."

There are two ways in which the world-traveler comes to experience the true realities of the world. First, he experiences difficulties and struggles and he becomes involved in distressing incidents during his travels. Although these are a relatively small part of the total range of travel experiences, their bare existence

Africa Leaking

Bamako, Mali

FINALLY, WE ARRIVED at a boutique hotel managed by a French-American couple in Bamako. At last, we had running hot water and fresh-smelling towels, a soft bed and nice linens. For a second, we almost thought we had left Africa.

But in the early morning – *always* in the early morning – we were banged on the head (literally!) back to reality. We were awoken by loud bangs on the walls above our heads. I opened the hotel-room door to see a couple of technicians working – yet again – on a broken toilet on the other side of the wall. This had happened many other times during our travels around the African continent. "Can't you repair it later?!" I exclaimed, half asleep and fully desperate. "Don't you see we are sleeping? It's 6:00 am!" "There's a big leak," one of them mumbled.

Leak! ... "In the beginning was the Word," the divine sound that put everything in place, and a new Creation became possible. There's always a Word that reorganizes the universe anew, and deepens one's understanding of peoples and places, circumstances and countries. This time around, I happened to get it from a plumber at 6:00 am.

Leak! ... and suddenly there was *Light!* Around this magical voodoo word, the whole continent began to restructure and mold itself into new shapes and forms. The Darkness of Africa, the Mystery of Africa, the Puzzle of Africa all of a sudden became less impenetrable and everything began to fall into place.

Now I understood! It's because of leaks that the toilet tanks never have water in Africa. This explains the permanent puddles of water under the toilet bowls. Likewise, the pipe that is supposed to take the water to the showerhead leaks and the water dissipates under the floor of the bathroom – that is why it is always damp and smelly. And of course, the drinking water never makes it to the reservoir and that's why there's never any drinking water.

Suddenly, the Divine Word begins to encompass all, shedding its light on all mysteries...

The electricity never reaches your room because an electric wire was chewed somewhere by a hungry rat and the current leaks – beware of electrical shocks! And with no electricity flowing through the wires, the fridge begins to leak, and the meat rots, and the fridge goes on leaking and leaking, until it is no fridge anymore, but rather a sad white box that turns into a storage for hot Cokes and pea tins.

Then it rains – a big tropical rain. The roof has just three holes but they get bigger with every downpour. And the roof starts leaking and you are swimming in your house or paddling with a canoe.

Africa leaking ...

The thirty-year-old Mercedes taxi cannot start because the battery is leaking. And when you finally get a group of youngsters to push, and it starts moving again, then the engine starts leaking and the oil never reaches the motor. But if you get lucky and it starts moving again, then there's another, more insidious and stealthy leak – *air!* Air is constantly leaking from all the tires of all the cars throughout the continent. Sometimes with a bang, sometimes with a whimper, a tire will definitely go flat before you reach your next destination. Half of Africa is busy changing tires, while the other half is busy collecting the inner tires, dipping them in a bucket of water, and trying to find the leaking holes to mend.

And just when some glimmer of hope appears on the horizon, when a well-educated politician from one of the best families in the country appears, with all the promise of fairness, good governance, and true democracy, just when all the ballot boxes are in place and a new beginning seems once again a possibility, the by-now-ruthless word intervenes again to destroy all hope: *The ballot boxes begin to leak!* Votes go in but don't stay in. Termites and other strange animals start chewing the boxes, and the votes leak out and disappear into the sewage system of African political life. And there's nothing you can do.

You can't go to the banks to get your money and leave Africa for good: for when ballot boxes begin to leak, the banks start leaking too (together with the wealth of Africa). And there is no money, no economy, no functioning state. You are stuck. Stuck in Africa. For the rest of your life, condemned to watch everything leak.

And leak. And leak. And leak…

must be acknowledged, accommodated, and, finally, embraced. Second, there are the ugly and unpleasant realities of the world and its peoples. We may call this the grand aspect of the disturbing realities of the world. Part of this grand aspect is more immediate and attacks our senses directly: the ugly sights, sounds, or smells that are the result of human actions—for one cannot speak of an "ugly landscape" or of a "disturbing mountain"; nature itself is neutral, and at most, one may speak of a boring or unvaried landscape. However, the most important of these unpleasant realities are the injustices, the inequalities, the poverty we encounter in the world. These realities are part of the world's fabric. The traveler must learn to *accept* the annoying incidents in the journey and the unpleasant realities of the world as constituting the dark side of the bipolar reality of existence. He must then go a step further: instead of judging, rejecting, or avoiding contact with them, he should consciously and intentionally embrace them. The more he does so, the more he will gradually discover that they become a springboard propelling him deeper into all facets of the world. Let us now examine in more detail these two types of challenges the traveler must necessarily always face.

Difficulties and Struggles

Traveling around the world is not easy. Many difficulties must be met and many problems must be solved on a daily basis. A number of challenging situations arise every now and then, some of which include human conflicts or arguments. The range of unpleasant situations is wide: from ordinary and common occurrences such as missing a bus and having to wait an extra day for the next, to a heated argument with a boatman who has attempted to cheat you. Sometimes the food at a restaurant is horrible, a hotel room is dirty, or your bed is uncomfortable. Occasionally, you might need to struggle with an official who tries to use his power against you; at other times, you may have to hold your own on a matter of principle. The list of potential problems is as infinite as the variety of possible life situa-

*Contrast I:
A float of Simon Bolivar, the father of South America, after the extravagant Rio Carnival Parade, with a favela (shantytown) in the background. Rio de Janeiro, Brazil.*

tions. Yet each difficulty and problem may be transformed into a unique opportunity to deepen one's understanding of the culture one is in, and to strengthen one's mental and psychological reserve. Often, challenges are best met with a dose of humor and a light-hearted attitude. **[Africa Leaking]** By considering each difficulty that arises as an opportunity to learn something that is impossible to learn in any other way, one may begin to welcome it rather than shrink back from it.

When the journey has finally finished and the traveler reflects upon his moments of difficulty or even despair, he will realize that it is those more than any others that led to the most transformative experiences and which helped him delve deeper into the foreign cultures and himself. As the Sri Aurobindo quote in the beginning of this section states, there is a universal principle at work whereby the difficulties one has to solve are proportionate to the things one must learn. The more rare and novel the difficulties, the more precious and long-lasting the gifts they bear. Every difficulty can teach us something new about ourselves and our relationships with other people. Through tangled and complicated situations, we are forced to become more awake and muster the totality of our energies and capabilities, channeling them into new fields of action and play. In so doing, we come to touch the world at points we never knew existed.

Difficulties come in many forms and shapes. During one's travels, repeated minor irritations may hold the key to new and more all-encompassing lessons to be learned. Even outright conflicts are part of life and may reveal meanings that become obvious only later. **[Vietcong Fighter]** The traveler, emboldened by the realization that there is a gift at the center of every real or imaginary disaster, may even occasionally go with the flow *without resisting* the events that appear to lead

Contrast II:
A gold-jewelry
salesman walking
on a sewage pipe
through garbage
in the slums.
Mumbai, India.

him into what seems to be a difficult situation. He might even consent to a strange convergence of circumstances steering him into the path of a hurricane for the first time in his life. **[Wilma]**

The Ugly and Unpleasant Realities of the World

The traveler is not just out to cherry-pick the beautiful and pleasant elements of the world. Natural beauty and wonders, great cities, picturesque villages, majestic ceremonies, unique fiestas, and cultural events ought to be central in one's exploration. Yet all these things are what they are by virtue of the existence of their opposites. Stunning landscapes exist as such because of their contrast to boring or uninteresting ones. Beautiful cities and villages are judged as being so because they are compared with the ugly cities and non-picturesque villages that outnumber them.

The mutual dependence of ugliness and beauty, pleasantness and unpleasantness, makes our world what it is. *Interdependent origination* is actually one of the central tenets of Buddhist philosophy. It is the notion that nothing possesses its own irreducible self-nature, but everything depends on something else for its existence. These interdependent opposites are the building blocks from which our world is constructed. It is meaningless, if not impossible, to attempt to shy away from the negative pole of reality. That said, most things in the world lie between the spaces defined by the extreme opposites and include qualities of both. One may thus cultivate the ability to see qualities of beauty and harmony in things that seem ugly or imperfect.

Vietcong Fighter

Cu Chi, Vietnam

I had already been cheated many times across the whole spectrum of my dealings with the Vietnamese. Taxi drivers, hotel managers, and fruit sellers were overcharging me at every possible opportunity. Being an experienced traveler, I was amazed at how I was being exploited like a novice every time I slightly dropped my guard. All the daily little robberies, exploitations, and occasional bullying by the Vietnamese are effective because the majority of tourists allow it. Visitors come to Vietnam to have a good time, and they don't want to constantly argue about the price of everything. Most of the time, the points of contention and the amounts of money involved are insignificant – a visitor does not want to spoil his good mood over a dollar, so he easily gives in. However, big or small, these amounts and their related daily skirmishes have an additive effect that turns out to be quite annoying. After several cheating incidents, I was searching for an opportunity to get even. In reality, I could never *truly* get even, as I was losing on all fronts! But I could at least choose one instance in which I would put up fierce resistance and come out on top.

The opportunity arose when I visited the military Cu Chi Tunnels of the Vietcong, situated in a forest 55 kilometers from Saigon. After having toured the elaborate tunnels and rooms of this small subterranean town, and after marveling at the many impressive traps and deceptive devices of the Vietcong, I bought my green Vietcong military hat from the souvenir shop and headed for my taxi. I had hired the taxi in Saigon after much negotiation, for an agreed-upon price of $27 round-trip, which also included the waiting time. As soon as I entered the taxi to head back to Saigon, the inevitable happened: the driver showed me a piece of paper with "40" written on it. He proceeded to explain, with minimal English and lots of hand gestures, that he had undercharged me, and now he wanted $40.

The moment I saw the paper requesting that I pay 50 percent above our agreed price, I knew that this was my golden opportunity to pay absolutely nothing and thus prove to the taxi driver, the whole Vietnamese nation, all the cheated visitors, and most importantly to myself, that *I too* was capable of the same Vietcong deception and guerilla tactics! If someone wants to cheat me, I can return the favor. Having felt the fighting spirit of the heroic Vietcong a few minutes earlier in the tunnels and with my new green military hat tightly perched on my oversized head, I was ready for a fierce battle to the bitter end.

First, like a noble warrior about to enter the battle, I offered him the chance to avoid the conflict: I presented the original piece of paper with the agreed upon price of $27 in his own writing. He nodded in disapproval waving his new piece of paper with the number "40." He then pointed to the car door, motioning for me to get out if I did not want to pay this amount. What?! Has he forgotten that I haven't paid him yet, and that if I got out of the car he would get nothing? I gave him a last chance: I said, "I will leave and not return." He did not respond. I opened the door, got out of the car, waved bye-bye, gave him the ironic smile of a combatant ready for battle, and headed towards the dense forest.

As I was going deeper into the forest, he realized his gaffe. It took him a couple of minutes to truly absorb the seriousness of his predicament: seeing a tourist leave without having paid him a dime! He drove his car into the forest to obstruct my path. I kept on walking, ignoring him. He got out of the car and started pulling my arm to stop me from walking further.

I pushed him back, showing fearlessness and willingness to fight. He started screaming at me. I screamed back.

Overhearing us, the nearby soldiers working at the Cu Chi Tunnels gathered to see what was going on. At that moment, he shrank back from the fight and offered to accept the original agreement. Having probably used similar methods with success for many years, he was not prepared for my shocking response: "No! No money!" As I said that, I walked, accompanied by the soldiers, towards the entrance kiosk, in order to wage my battle in public view.

In a few minutes, the taxi driver and I were arguing in front of a full audience of soldiers. I was determined to show all of my Vietcong qualities that were now magically surging to the surface from some hidden crypt within me. I had just displayed determination, fighting spirit, and courage. Now I had to show ruthlessness, ability to deceive, and advanced skills at maneuvering and hunting down the enemy!

The driver told them that I had paid nothing and that he wanted his money. "What do you say?" I screamed, staring straight in the eyes of the soldiers who had gathered around us. *"I have already paid you $15 for the single journey!"* (of course, this was a lie). I then presented my story, an amalgam of true and false information: We had agreed on $30, I had paid him $15 in advance, and now he wanted $45. He had demanded that I get out of the car, which I had, and now he was unhappy that I was going to pay him nothing more.

The taxi driver was dumbfounded. He looked at me with pleading eyes, but I stared back at him with a grin signifying that I was now playing his game, and playing it better than him. The taxi driver said that the agreement was for $27 and he was willing to honor it. The soldiers were completely baffled, not least because we both looked and sounded so convincing.

There was only one English speaker in the group of soldiers, and he now began to take his duty as both an interpreter and mediator in the conflict seriously. He told me that the taxi driver was finally willing to take me back with any price I would pay. I responded that I was willing to pay him *zero*, and that under no circumstances was I going to return with him, as he had already shown aggressive behavior. The interpreter, after admitting he didn't know who was telling the truth, suggested that we both go to the nearest police station to sort things out. I refused, insisting that I would never enter that taxi again. This led to a complete stalemate.

The soldiers then called the army officers, some of whom seemed to be Vietcong veterans. They arrived at the scene, and new discussions began. In a completely relaxed manner, I found a chair, sat down, and waited. I also emphasized that I would rather sleep in the camp than return with *this* taxi driver. In that moment, the driver realized that he had lost the game and tried to minimize his losses by asking the interpreter to tell me that he was a poor man with a big family and if I could give him another $5 or $10. Of course, this was one more of the innumerable tricks employed by many Vietnamese who deal with tourists. "Poor or rich," I said, "this man is a thief, and I am paying nothing more. I have already given him $15!" In a last desperate move, the driver lunged at me, threatening to hit me, when one of the officers grabbed him by the arm and yelled at him to get in his car and get lost. The same military officer then told me that the soldiers would drive me to the main road in a military jeep, where I could find another car to take me back to Saigon. This is what finally happened.

Here I was, in the heart of a true battlefield that had seen so much real heroic combat, giving my own little battle in full view of young soldiers as well as veteran Vietcong officers — and coming out on top! It definitely wasn't like the heroic battles of the past with real guns, blood, thunder, and death. It was just an insignificant skirmish that happened to be enacted on an historic battleground. However, when I realized victory was turning my way, I had the strange feeling that the spirit of the place had worked its way through me, endowing me with all the qualities of the fearless Vietcong fighters. I had just won a battle in the holiest of battlegrounds, using many of the methods the Vietcong had used against the US military. Somehow, the spirit of those warriors was reborn through me, even though my bloodless quarrel paled in comparison to their achievements. I felt I was honoring them in a most palpable manner and that the ripples of my little personal victory would have a lasting and universal effect. From now on, the taxi driver, and all the others with whom he would share the story, would think twice before trying to cheat a visitor again. *My battle was fought on behalf of all visitors in Vietnam — past and future.*

Yes, I am a modern Don Quixote! Yet how many of the thousand chivalrous battles of the Middle Ages does humanity recall? Which of those battles among knights and nobles and kings have become ingrained forever in the memory of the world? A mere handful. In the end, it is the funny, awkward, childish "battles" of the literary Don Quixote that have become the archetype of that lost heroic past. For in Don Quixote, one can see in all its purity and clarity that each memorable battle has a noble cause behind it, and that all battles are nothing but a game, or rather, a faint reflection of some ideal archetypal heroic feat we all carry in the innermost recesses of our soul.

While it is a matter of simple rationality to accept the reality and even the necessity of ugliness in the world, it is extremely difficult to bear the sight of children begging or of people living in countries with less freedom and fewer opportunities than what we are accustomed to. It is not easy to accept these realities simply by virtue of their interdependence on their opposites. As moral beings we revolt and want to put things right. We believe that it is possible to eradicate human injustices and extinguish poverty, disease, and oppression. When faced with such harsh realities, we may take it upon ourselves to change the world, which is a legitimate undertaking. However, the traveler cannot do this while he travels. If he decides that he must become involved in such noble pursuits, this must be done after his travels. Traveling is a work unto itself. It is impossible to introduce such grand endeavors in one's life while on the move.

But let us not sidetrack into a discussion of the big problems of humanity and how they can be eradicated. Instead, let us examine what attitude the traveler ought to adopt towards the unpleasant realities and ugliness in the world, and with what frame of mind he may confront them.

Equality

> *For the universal soul all things and all contacts of things carry in them an essence of delight best described by the Sanskrit aesthetic term "rasa," which means at once sap or essence of a thing and its taste. It is because we do not seek the essence of the thing in its contact with us, but look only to the manner in which it affects our*

desires and fears, our cravings and shrinkings, that grief and pain, imperfect and transient pleasure or indifference, that is to say, blank inability to seize the essence, are the forms taken by the Rasa. If we could be entirely disinterested in mind and heart and impose that detachment on the nervous being, the progressive elimination of these imperfect and perverse forms of Rasa would be possible and the true essential taste of the inalienable delight of existence in all its variations would be within our reach.

— Sri Aurobindo

It is difficult to bear the unpleasant sensations that violently attack our senses, such as a foul smell, a disturbing sound, or the urban pollution that steals the air we breathe. When it comes to sights, unpleasant sensations exist on an even grander scale: a street full of uncollected garbage in Naples; a poor shantytown in the outskirts of Rio de Janeiro; the ugly, overdeveloped waterfront of a Spanish coastal town set against an otherwise pristine backdrop of crystal clear waters—all of them are disturbing and painful sights, the unfortunate results of human actions.

In order to confront these unpleasant sensations of the world, we must adopt the attitude of *equality* towards all sensations. We must force all of our senses to experience everything in its raw form, without any interference from the analytical and judging functions of the mind. Yogis have been practicing equality towards all sensations for millennia. The idea is to capture the *rasa*, the substance, the existential quality of each and every sensation, without the mind immediately superimposing a judgment on it. All sensations are equal *as sensations* inasmuch as they are variations on an infinite spectrum of sensations.

It is not easy to smell a foul odor and not react in disgust or make the characteristic involuntary grimace. Yet it is only by refraining from reacting in this way that one may experience the foul smell in an unmediated, direct manner. A foul smell is still a smell of a very special kind that is interesting exactly because it is new and unique. [Chòu Dòufu] It is only through a willful exertion that one may begin to see the world as it truly is and not through the filters of one's upbringing, prejudices, and already formed tastes. By forcing our mind to stand back, we may return to the primal mode of experiencing our world, like a newborn, who sees and feels everything with a freshness and intensity, unblemished by the clouding of mental judgments.

Deferral of Judgment

Related to the above, there is an important mindset that eases our confrontation with the world's unpleasant realities and facilitates the attainment of equality. We may call it *deferral of judgment*. This term is often used to denote refraining from judging human behavior, but this meaning is too narrow. Here we mean some-

Wilma

For what the Spirit sees, creates a Truth,
and what the soul imagines is made a World
                    — Sri Aurobindo

Cancun, Mexico

MY ITINERARY SAID: "20th of October – Travel to Cancun via Chichen Itza." Cancun: the latest tourist capital of Mexico. Chichen Itza: the first Mayan ruins I was about to visit. I entered a taxi.

Ten minutes later, as if remembering something important he ought to have told me earlier, the taxi driver said in broken English: "You sure want go Cancun? Hurricane go there!" He turned around, picked up a newspaper from the back seat, and handed it to me. I couldn't believe my eyes: A huge, impressive color photo covered half the front page. It looked like an enormous spiral galaxy, just like the one in which our solar system is situated! "That's Wilma," he said. "Wilma, the galaxy?" I almost replied. "Wilma, big hurricane!" he added with emphasis. Well, the main title below was perfectly clear: "Wilma viene con furia!" ("Wilma approaches with fury!") "But no problem," the driver continued, in an attempt not to lose the ride. "Not exactly pass over Cancun. Centro Wilma will be 10 kilometros in the sea, in Gulf of Mexico. Expertos say she hit tonight," he said in broken English well-spoken.

It took me a few minutes to quite absorb it. Here I was, heading towards Cancun on the same day that a huge spiral galaxy decided to make its way to the same location. What was this? I could not rationalize, for suddenly I started imagining myself moving from the edges of our galaxy towards its center. "If only the center wouldn't be in the ocean," I almost mumbled to myself. And then I spit it out: "Well, let's go then!" I couldn't believe my own ears – did *I* just say that?!

I already felt it; the invisible forces that compelled me were beyond my control. In one of those rare moments in life, I started seeing fate spinning its web around my days. Yet this was no ordinary fate – it was a truly God-sent gift. Wilma was traveling to meet me. *A real hurricane!* Coming from a Mediterranean island, I had never experienced one. I had only seen its distant images and faint echoes on TV. Was it a coincidence that I had just finished reading the book *The Darkness of God*, which explored the antinomian nature of Yahweh, the Jewish God? And was it a coincidence that on this same day, on the way to Cancun, I would see the fearful sculpted images of Chac, the Mayan god of thunder and rain, covering the walls of the temples in Chichen Itza? Chac, with his long curling snout, reptilian eyes, and huge scary fangs, was a potent and palpable reminder of the dark side of Yahweh.

My deepest wishes were not to remain unfulfilled. For, as it often happens, the weather experts and the taxi driver were wrong. A few hours after I had checked into a hotel in Cancun, the latest news was that Wilma had slightly shifted her course, and her center would pass over the town. I already had the feeling that I was truly approaching the center of our galaxy. My hotel, where I was to be willingly trapped for the next five days, had the most interesting and odd space-travelers! I had never met such a fascinating collection of characters in my life up to that point or since: There was a drug-dealer-turned-Christian-missionary (the only other person apart from me who was fascinated by the prospect of enjoying the spectacle); a Ukrainian couple who had emigrated to the United States after traveling around the world; a group of young Russian Staroveris (Old-Believers) living in Oregon, USA – with the men wearing long beards and the women head-scarves; one of the 1,500 inhabitants of Norfolk Island in the South Pacific; a Jew from Munich; a Swiss professor who seemed to have all the possible survival skills and equipment; Carlos the crazy Mexican—the list had no end.

Wilma was a little late, but faithful to our predestined meeting. And what an encounter it was! At midnight on the 21st, she hit with all her mighty destructive force. And I was right in her center, elated to *see, hear, and feel* the divine force that moves the cosmos. I could see it transforming itself into mighty thunder, torrential rain, powerful winds that felled trees like matchsticks. But above all, I felt Wilma on my bare skin. Like her lover, I stood alone in the street and let the wind carry me aside. I went outside to the hotel's open courtyard and let the pouring rain soak me. I approached the bending branches of the huge palm tree and felt Wilma's overpowering strength consume me.

But that is not all. For Wilma also introduced me to the mystery of the darkness of God—the destructive power of the divine that is sometimes called *the wrath of God*. For the power that runs the show of our lives is a two-headed entity: With one head it destroys so that with the other it may create anew. Destruction is the foundation of the never-ending creative process that renews itself out of its own bipolar nature. The Jewish Yahweh, to whose irrational might the biblical Job was to bow, would be forever united in my imagination with the Mayan god of thunder and rain, Chac. Bearing so many different names, the god of destruction, decomposition, decay, chaos, would show me his frightful fangs in the heart of the Mayan World, where some of his most magnificent temples were constructed to honor him for all eternity.

Yet not for a second did I feel any fear. Quite the contrary; I was dazzled by the beauty of this force, the magnitude of which I had never before experienced. I was mesmerized by its infinite potential to destroy. I was overwhelmed by the simplicity, even the harmony, of its destructive might, which at times seemed to create works of art and music of infinite depth, of which our eyes can see but a small part and to which our ears can only imperfectly attune.

The center of the galaxy came to me.

Chac showed me his mighty fangs.

Wilma and I met, bonded, and parted.

thing much more general that encompasses not only refraining from judging local behavior, but also from judging the architecture and aesthetics of a country, the tastes of its food, the sounds of its music. We are talking about the deferral of judgment regarding *everything* experienced in the local culture.

It is most difficult to overcome our instinctive tendency to label everything, in itself a form of judgment. Our mind takes over without our consent and we automatically attach a label to every form, sensation, situation. Instant labeling leads to categorization, which makes us think that we know something just because we have put it in our mental bookshelf of categories. Sometimes we even confuse this supposed knowing with understanding. However, neither knowing nor understanding is equivalent to experiencing. All sensations, for example, may be felt by the body through the agency of the mind. But the mind itself, although necessary, is not sufficient to reproduce them—our senses are indispensable. There is an immediacy in sensation itself that is due to the actual contact of our senses with the world. A sensation may become a concept, but the concept itself is not a substitute for the sensation. The experience of every sensation is of another mode of being than the word that communicates it. Yet this labeling process, which applies to everything, not just to sensations, and which also understandably has its own proper place and function in life, is the greatest block to experiencing the world in its purest mode.

When it comes to human behavior itself, the deferral of judgment becomes a traveler's golden rule. In India we might see a procession of self-mutilating worshipers with spears going through their torsos and faces and think that they are crazy. Rather, we must view this as an opportunity to acknowledge that, while we do not understand their behavior, we see it for what it is and later try to learn about it. We will then discover that there is something much deeper going on that relates to spiritual practice. To take another example, on the way to explore the Hamar tribe in Ethiopia's South Omo Valley, we may come upon a market at which locals invite us to witness the young men's rite of passage featuring ritual whipping, by which young men prove their manly abilities and are permitted to claim a wife and start a family. We end up in the forest witnessing a few handsome teenagers whipping female family members on their backs until they bleed. It is easy to rush into premature conclusions and think that this behavior is the product of a violent male-dominated society. Yet if we defer judgment and are attentive, we will observe that the women are actually willing participants and persistently *demand* that they be whipped! Rather than judging, we may seek to better understand the situation by unabashedly asking the locals to enlighten us, and by reading about the custom later. As it turns out, the custom serves a deeper purpose: that of strengthening familial bonds and of initiating young men and women into adulthood. It is such behaviors that do not make sense to us that are actually the surest and fastest way to understanding new cultures—for they reveal their most crucial and unique secrets; their real soul.

From the Answer to the Question

Our educational systems, the way we are brought up, even our whole society, revolve around the concept of the Answer. The way we understand education, our exams and evaluation systems, depend on finding the correct answer to a question. The question is always provided, handed out for free. It is a given.

Yet in actual life as well as in thought, the Question is almost always more important than the Answer. Not only does it come before the latter, logically and temporally, but, in a sense, it molds and determines it. It creates the substratum, the context in which any answer may exist. Most often it includes a part of the answer, since it delineates the sphere of possible answers it requests. Without the proper questions, answers become irrelevant, incoherent, or weak. It is the Question that empowers, directs, and guides the whole movement from ignorance to knowledge. Every question may be considered the beginning, the *prerequisite* of the search for knowledge. Every answer may be considered the *fruition* of a question.

Although there is usually one or a small number of correct answers, there are an infinite number of possible ways for a question to be conceived and then formulated. This is one of the main reasons there are no exams for formulating the right questions. Yet finding and formulating the relevant questions to any particular circumstance is one of the most important tasks in life. All knowledge is the product of a set of questions thoughtfully conceived and verbally expressed. Our philosophy, our sciences, even our arts, have their origins in crucial questions that arose in the minds of certain people.

Conceiving the proper question and then finding the appropriate way to formulate it lies at the heart of the way we learn naturally and the way we understand the world and our place in it. It is the lack of the right questions in one's life that is at the root of our Kafkaesque contemporary alienation—not the lack of answers. We have no answers because we have no questions!

Redirecting one's focus from finding the right answers to formulating the proper questions about a few central issues of life is the most important element in realigning one's actions with one's true nature. It is the questions that propel our lives, that define who we will become and what we will create.

Travel—more than any other activity—cultivates the art of asking questions. The traveler is constantly immersed in unknown worlds and bears witness to thousands of incidents that he struggles to decipher for the first time. He begins to see everything with the wonder and inquisitiveness of a child. In the same way a child incessantly asks questions to make sense of the world, the traveler is continually immersed in a sea of potential questions he must give voice to, and then properly formulate, in order to make sense of his experiences: How can an arid desert exist next to the lush rainforest of Peru? How can live fish in tanks be sold in the farmers' markets in the highlands of China if there is no river or sea nearby? Why didn't Buddhism flourish in India, the country of its origin? It is through questions such as these that the world begins to unravel its needlework and reveal its secrets. Just like a child trying to grasp the various threads of knowledge to comprehend their interconnectedness, the traveler continually reweaves his new experiences into a constantly changing tapestry of the world.

The shift from a world of answers to a world of questions, which mirrors a shift from the world of adults to the world of children, might be termed The Second Ignorance—it is a transition from a world we thought we knew and understood to a new world we see for the first time and of which we know very little. The traveler is permanently immersed in a world of questions that urgently demand answers. It is this healthy craving and desire that turns the wheel of travel. The degree that we allow the world of questions to become predominant in our

Defer Judgment I: Hurting the body for the sake of the soul. Procession with self-mutilating worshipers. Tiruchirappalli, Tamil Nadu, India.

life is the degree to which our journey and our life will become infused with a new innocence and excitement.

On Planning and Spontaneity

Long-term travel needs planning if one intends to thoroughly explore a country. One must read about the geographical zones of the region, its flora and fauna, its natural beauties and wonders, and, above all, its history, culture, and customs. Studying must then be accompanied by actually forming a tentative itinerary and a route on the map, and planning one's mode of travel at each different section. Without careful travel preparation and study, one's experiences will remain shallow and one's journey will move along a thin surface of sensations and impressions, with no key to their understanding. Visiting a Muslim country without having read anything about Islam, or visiting Tibet without having studied some Buddhism or the county's recent history, is like entering a modern art museum without ever having read anything about Picasso. Study ought to begin before one travels, but must also continue during travel. After gaining an acquaintance with the new culture, many new questions arise, the answers to which deepen one's understanding of the new place. It is only by studying and asking questions that one can hope to unravel the myriad aspects of the world.

However, although planning and organization are indispensable to travel, they must not become so rigid as to preclude spontaneity and the freedom to re-plan or even completely alter one's travel itinerary. One must always be open to suggestions for new places to visit, whether they come from locals or other travel-

Defer Judgment II: A Hamar youth whipping female family members. South Omo Valley, Ethiopia.

ers (usually traveling in the opposite direction). One must find a balance between preplanning and the freedom to alter one's route. A region that initially seemed interesting and rich in attractions might prove to be unworthy of any further exploration, while a region to which we had originally allocated only a few days may end up deserving a week or more. We might find that a festival we must not miss is starting in a nearby town in a few days, in which case we may alter both our route and our time spent in the region. In another instance, we may befriend a local family or a fellow traveler and decide to stay longer at a place to enjoy the hospitality or to change our route to be with our new friend.

Of all the things that may lead us to change our itinerary, the most common is actually falling in love with a place and deciding to get more of it. One reason that a long-term journey usually ends up being a longer-term journey—often much longer than originally planned—is the fact that we cannot really skip places we don't like (because we don't know that until we get there), yet we can always extend our time in places we come to love. Often, we may be so awestruck by the natural beauty of a country or by the otherworldliness of a new culture that an invisible force impels us to stay longer.

Altering one's plans or route, however, is not the only thing meant by spontaneity. Spontaneity should be an integral part of the traveler's mindset. It signifies the readiness to act or react in an unplanned, impulsive manner to the new discoveries of the journey: We may be exploring a Tarahumara Indian village in Mexico, under the sweltering sun. To cool off, we buy an ice cream and we realize that a few locals sitting nearby are lustfully staring at our ice cream, which they cannot themselves afford. With an impromptu gesture, we decide to buy them

Chóu Dóufu

*You are a foreigner in a foreign land. You must learn to hate
what this city hates and to love what it loves.*
— from *Oedipus at Colonus* by Sophocles

Shanghai, China

I HAD ALREADY BEEN IN CHINA for more than a month when I entered the restored and touristy Yuyuan area of the old town of Shanghai. After a brief stroll around the overcrowded streets full of market stalls and eateries, I smelled "that strange smell" that seemed to follow me everywhere and whose source still eluded me. When I first smelled it, I was in Beijing, and I thought it came from some nearby broken sewage pipe, for that was the closest match my brain could find in my mental library of world smells. Sewage stinks of sewage, yet this odor was quite distinct and different from what I was accustomed to—something I attributed to, well, the different composition of Chinese excrement! Later on, when I encountered the same smell in other towns such as Xi'an, I realized that the sewage-pipe-hypothesis had a hole, for it became apparent that not all broken sewage pipes could have possibly exuded the same type of unpleasant smell.

This time in Shanghai, I decided to solve the mystery. Like a hunting dog, I started sniffing my way through the crowds, trying to move towards the direction in which the bad smell got stronger. After a while, ahead of me I saw a huge queue of Chinese. I followed the smell and I discovered that it led to a small food stall. As I approached, all my smell receptors turned bright red. To my surprise, I saw that the two servers were selling just one single product, which not only smelled but also looked like excrement!

"What the hell is this?" I asked a local in the queue.

"Tofu," he responded.

"This is not tofu," I said, "I have eaten tofu—this is not how it looks and definitely not how it smells!"

"No, this is *chóu dóufu*, stinky tofu," added another guy behind who had overheard the conversation.

"Well, like hell it stinks," I said.

"Yes, but *very* tasty," the guy behind added with a big smile.

At that moment, the Travel Genie appeared above me and whispered, "You cannot not discover *why* all these people wait here for half an hour to eat this thing. You have to try it!" So there I was, joining in the queue like a hungry, smell-struck Chinese, waiting for someone to serve me a piece of shit on a paper plate!

The first bite was nothing special. For the second bite, I brought the tofu to my nose and smelled it up close. I realized that the smell-from-afar was very different from the near-smell, which did not smell foul at all. Actually, it was rather interesting, at least by virtue of being simply a new smell I had never encountered. It was now obvious that the smell-from-afar was the composite of the frying process and the un-fried tofu. The finished cooked product exuded another smell. I actually realized that the taste and near-smell of the fermented tofu were in harmony. Upon further exploration with nose and tongue, I slowly began to discover more layers of aroma that were not initially discernible. Gradually, I discarded my initial negative stance towards this new food and accepted that it was actually quite tasty. It also left an aftertaste that left me wanting for more (in the same way, say, a chocolate does). After eating the whole thing, I returned to the kiosk. During this second round, just as I was eating the freshly fried new portion, I suddenly had a strange sensation: This thing was really good. I mean *really, really good!*

As I was eating the fifth portion, I was already in heaven. Standing in the most touristy place of Shanghai, I had an epiphany with pieces of stinky tofu that I could not stop devouring. I know the word "epiphany" is often used to describe religious experiences rather than carnal pleasures of the lowest form, but since I cannot find an expression more appropriate, I will go ahead and say it: I had a *culinary awakening* that sparked within me a deep appreciation for the Chinese cuisine and the inexhaustibly imaginative Chinese mind and nose.

Gradually, after a few times of eating fermented tofu in other places in China, I began to truly identify the smell with the incredible taste that I had now come to adore. What was earlier experienced as foul began to register in my mind as a pleasurable smell—if for no other reason than that it led me to the place where I could buy my beloved tofu.

The acquiring of new tastes is akin to the extension of the senses. For suddenly you discover that the range within which your senses registered was extremely limited, and that when transposed into a new field of sensory inputs, into new worlds with different patterns of tastes, music, or art, they naturally expand to accommodate the new.

The fermented tofu incident was to be followed by similar experiences. Initially repulsive smells ended up holding the key to new worlds I never could have imagined existed. When I would later fall in love with durian in Thailand or with stinky cheeses in France, I would always recall the moment of my very first culinary awakening—an awakening that is probably only possible in China.

some ice cream so that we can all enjoy it together. **[No Thanks, But Thanks]** We may be visiting the Sri Ramana Maharshi ashram in Arunachala, India, a day before the monthly Giri Pradakshina festival, in which case we spontaneously decide to join the pilgrims and circumambulate the nearby Arunachala hill in the heat of the day, becoming Hindu pilgrims ourselves, if only for a day. We may be in Ternate, Indonesia, during the month of Ramadan when, early one morning, we are awoken by deafening music. Upon inquiring, we discover a centuries-old tradition: High school and university students move from one neighborhood to another in trucks carrying huge loudspeakers and singing religious songs to wake up the faithful for the early morning prayer. What would be more natural than to… climb on the truck and join the team in order to experience the living tradition and have a unique interaction with Muslim youth!

These examples give an idea of the kind of spontaneous reactions a traveler may have as a result of his free-flowing interaction with the cultures he is immersed in. Joining the pilgrims for the Giri Pradakshina or waking up the Muslim faithful from a truck filled with students may be rare and extreme instances of spontaneity that only happen a few times in one's journey. Yet it is by being constantly mindful of such possibilities and being open to altering one's plans that one may experience such unforgettable moments. While organization, planning, and study are indispensable parts of travel, the peak experiences of our travels usually end up being these unplanned moments when, surrendering to the surprising gifts of life, we allow ourselves to be carried away by the stream of unexpected events that converge on our path.

C. THE TRAVEL MODE OF BEING

While traveling, one enters into another mode of being. The way he thinks and behaves becomes so transformed that he may be said to have been transposed to another dimension. It is not easy to describe this travel mode of being because it is comprised of many different experiential components that are intertwined. To express them in language will already be distorting their experiential nature. Still, we may attempt to somehow delineate or circumscribe this mode of being by examining some of its strongest and most evident elements.

The Traveler-Hermit and the Inner Journey

It might be strange to compare the life of a world-traveler, who is on the move and interacting with thousands of people, with the life of a spiritual hermit. Yet, paradoxically, the two have more in common than meets the eye. Just as a hermit, the world-traveler is "alone" most of the time. Not in the ordinary sense of the word, for he is almost always surrounded by people. However, even while he interacts with the world, he does so more as a student of life than as a participant in the everyday socializing in which the majority of humanity is immersed. Thus, although the traveler is fully *in* the world, he is not *of* the world. His interactions have the character of those of an explorer, and they do not really take him out of his state of aloneness. But time-wise, these interactions are only a part of his life. When not traveling and interacting with people, he spends many hours a day reading and studying, just as a hermit does. Then he has to gather all his experiences, make sense of them, and reflect on their meaning and significance, just as a hermit meditates on the meaning and significance of his inner experiences. Finally, he has to allow all these new elements to act upon him and transform him into another person.

It is this element of inner transformation that makes the traveler and hermit so similar. While moving in the outer world, the traveler also works on his inner world. For the journey is always twofold—it has an outer and an inner aspect. The *outer journey* turns out to be an instrument that serves the much more important and central *inner journey*. Although the outer aspect is more easily communicable, the true content and meaning of the double journey becomes clear only when the

What would be more natural than to … climb on the truck and join the youth in their mission to wake up the faithful! Ternate, Indonesia.

inner dimension sheds its revealing light on the whole endeavor. Only after the outer events become part of a greater reality and find their place in the grander scheme of things does the traveler feel that something new and fresh has been gained.

This does not happen continuously. Sometimes, whole days or even weeks go by without the discovery of any true significance in the crowding facts of life-on-the-move. But then, unexpectedly, in moments of silence (and more rarely, *hermetic silence*), when one rests without any immediate aims or plans, when the mind is allowed to freely reshuffle and reassemble the multifarious experiences that came one's way, cracks begin to appear in the seemingly meaningless series of disconnected events, encounters, sensations, and feelings, from which bright rays of meaning slip in and illuminate the whole field of understanding. At other, rarer moments, the outer and inner dimensions are experienced simultaneously as a single entity, a torrential stream of meaning and substance that seeks to express itself in words that bring forth this deeper and often surprising unity. In such moments, the traveler may feel the need to take pen to paper and express his ideas, feelings, or the new discoveries he has made. These words become, in effect, the connecting thread between the outer and inner worlds, and thus the expression of the oneness of the two parallel journeys. That is why a traveler's writings may end up corresponding to the prayers of a hermit, being more or less an expression of the love and wonder of one's life-journey.

Thus the traveler is not only solitary in his quest, not only alone in his individual mode of experiencing the world, but he also lives largely in solitude, in as much as the final goal of his journey is none other than his inner transformation. In the end, the traveler, like the hermit, also ends up working on himself—albeit through

No Thanks, But Thanks

*On a superficial level, the giving of thanks is merely a social convention.
Its forms vary greatly. In some societies the absence of all verbal expressions
of thanks indicates not a lack of gratitude, but rather a deeper awareness
of mutual belonging than our society has. To the people in question, an
expression like "thank you" would seem as inappropriate as tipping family
members would seem to us.*

— David Steindl-Rast

Copper Canyon, Mexico

I BOUGHT ICE CREAM for a group of Tarahumara Indian women and their children who were weaving traditional baskets in front of the hotel. None of them thanked me. They didn't nod, didn't smile acknowledgingly. Some did not even raise their head to see the Greek bearing gifts! One of them glanced at the ice cream cup and with her left hand moved it closer without interrupting her work, as if to say "got it." Only after a few minutes did she stop her work in order to eat it. I couldn't figure out why she didn't eat it immediately – after all, ice cream melts quickly. Probably, she waited a bit longer in order to savor the moment. Still, her overall reaction was that of a woman showing that her daily job of weaving was more important than the surprise gift. When she finally started eating it, she became just as engaged with the new pleasure as she was previously with her work. Even though every single Western-type of thankfulness was absent, I somehow *felt* the women's gratitude through the absolute naturalness by which they received the gift as something ordinary, and through the way they were enjoying it in a most genuine manner.

Later on, I would encounter this same attitude and behavior in other parts of the world. In non-Christianized Papua, the locals would simply grab the gift abruptly from my hands and immediately share it (if it was food) or simply engage with it. In India, beggars would never nod or smile or say anything. In Ethiopia and Cameroon, kids would simply smile upon receiving something, and run to share their joy with others. In all these places, as I finally came to understand, thankfulness is implied in the acceptance of the gift or the helping gesture. Explicitly expressing one's thanks in words is unnecessary or meaningless for them.

Accepting a gift without verbal thanks is just one of the many social conventions a world-traveler comes to recognize. Many of the normal rules of propriety are culturally specific, yet we assume that our rules are universal since they have been ingrained in our psyche from a young age. We consider it normal to say a hundred *pleases* every day, even between family members, as if this word constitutes some type of magic spell permitting any transaction. We would never dare eat a bowl of rice with our bare hands, yet this is what people do in most Muslim countries as well as in India, the South Pacific, and many other places. We would never dare slurp our soup in front of others or spit in a crowded street, yet this is what the Chinese do and for good reasons – slurping allows more flavors to enter the nose, thus making the soup tastier, while spitting in a very polluted metropolis covered in smog is the minimum one can do to remain healthy. And of course, the Chinese do not say "sorry" when they touch you or push you lightly in order to overtake you in a crowded street or the train – can you imagine a billion Chinese saying a billion sorrys with every passing touch?!

It is actually through observation, understanding, and the final (partial or whole) adoption of foreign norms that the traveler first comes to understand the relativity of normalcy in human behavior. He also comes to realize the contingent nature of almost all the rules of propriety. These rules depend on the history and character of a nation, as well as the infinite random events that formed its culture through the ages.

When the traveler begins to feel comfortable adopting a behavior that goes against what he has learned, he also begins to experience a new sense of freedom. Nothing quite limits him again as it did before—for now he realizes that most social constraints are conventions passed from one generation to another without much thought. Upon returning home, the traveler may readopt his "normal" modes of behavior and respect his specific cultural norms. Yet these once-holy rules, which felt as if they had been carved on stone, will now seem like children's games. The returning traveler will feel that they have lost their solidity and even rationale.

an opposite movement outwards and through the world. The real job of both is self-work and self-transformation. The traveler is a hermit immersed in the world, just as a hermit is a spiritual traveler withdrawn from the world. **[Legs & Arms]**

Doing and Becoming

The dichotomy of the outer and inner journey is mirrored in another bipolarity that sheds further light on the travel mode of being: sedentary life pertains to Doing, whereas travel life pertains to Becoming.

A person living a normal life with a regular regimented timetable, a fixed place of residence and work, a routine taking care of family matters, and occasional holidays once or twice a year, is preoccupied with *doing* things. He *does* work, he *does* shopping, he *does* socializing. His daily program is full of things to do. Even if some time is put aside or stolen from other activities for a hobby or for studying and self-improvement, these activities are, as a rule, not central to a life immersed in society—they are a footnote in the margin of one's life.

Travel life is very different. The traveler has nothing *to do*. He may choose to sit on a bench in a park all day and simply observe the world pass by. Even while he explores places or interacts with foreign cultures or studies, there is nothing compulsory about these activities. There is nothing he *must* do or accomplish by some deadline (apart perhaps from some self-imposed but flexible date he may have set for himself to complete his exploration of a country).

However, although he is not working in the sense of having a conventional job, and is not doing anything by the usual standards of society, something else is actually going on: With every contact, event, experience that comes into his life, he is transformed. Even by simply wandering effortlessly between countries as a vagabond and interacting with the various people of different cultures or passively enjoying new landscapes, he opens himself to change. This is because just by mov-

Legs & Arms

Puno, Peru

MY WHITE LEGS: They stand out in the minibus of darker-colored ladinos and locals. How fat and strong they are! That's why Nature gave me strong legs: For one day I would travel around the world with them! But why weak arms? Now I know: They always get all the help they ask for. I never carry my suitcase from one place to another on my own — it's too heavy. There are always people around to help me. However, nobody can walk on my behalf.

Legs: the symbol of my solitude, my individual path, my uniqueness.

Arms: the symbol of togetherness, my connection to others, my belonging to the human race.

My legs make me who I am; they create my solitary path. My arms make me who I belong to; they connect me to the world.

My legs are the symbol of my strength and independent spirit. My arms are the symbol of my weakness and my dependent nature.

I look at my legs and see them marching onwards with the discipline of a soldier. I look at my arms and see them opening outwards, inviting all others to join me on the journey. I need my legs so that I may move on; I need my arms so that I may not forget that we all move on.

I use my arms, together with those offered by others, to load my suitcases onto the buses, taxis, and airplanes so that my legs can then take charge and move on. I begin, like in life itself, in togetherness, but I move in solitude. Then, I again end in togetherness, for I have to unload all my accumulated knowledge and experiences with the help of others, in order to count them as gains. After this, a new journey, a fresh cycle will start again.

Solitude and togetherness are intertwined. One cannot exist without the other. The more we find our own path in solitude, the more we connect to others when they appear in our lives — and they always do. Solitude is the prerequisite for true, authentic togetherness. For unless we discover ourselves, we cannot truly relate to others in depth.

Togetherness without solitude is the equivalent of meaninglessly loading and unloading one's luggage on a stationary bus. Togetherness then becomes an endless, self-repeating, burdensome immobility that feeds on its own need to sustain itself. This is, unfortunately, the commonest form of togetherness that binds many people. However, togetherness immersed in solitude propels itself to its own grander fulfillment. It is like loading the suitcases on the bus and moving on to the next town where some others will help unload. Togetherness then expands, extends, and multiplies, while moving along a never-ending ascending spiral.

Ascent is solitude. Togetherness, the spiral.

ing from place to place, he is by default in the school of life. Almost every interaction and experience of a traveler is unique and thus holds a power and value that surpasses anything a sedentary life has to offer. By being in the journey, the traveler ceases *to do* and is *becoming*.

Still, we must in the end acknowledge and accept the inescapable interconnectedness of the two: Becoming requires Doing, while Doing depends on the depth of the Becoming for whatever it creates. In our modern world, preoccupied

Traveler-hermit: A lone penguin returning home at sunset. Dunedin, New Zealand.

and obsessed with doing, it is good once in a while to redress the balance. If we were to take the side of Becoming, if only for a moment, and give it a sense of primacy with respect to Doing, we could say the following:

In order to *do* anything of value, one must first *become* able to do it. It is in this sense that Becoming is primary and Doing is secondary. It is who you are that creates what you do. The greatest people among us, whom we admire and venerate, first set out to become themselves; by becoming themselves, their doing became the fruition or expression of who they were. Beethoven's Ninth Symphony *is* Beethoven. His symphony is the real-life expression of his invisible becoming that preceded his composition. It is in this sense that we may in the end claim that Beethoven became his Ninth Symphony, just as Magellan became his journey, or Socrates, Confucius, and Jesus became their teachings. What they did in their lives was simply the living expression of who they first became.

Central Elements of the Becoming

One need only leave behind his daily routine and travel for a few months in order to enter and experience this mode of becoming. If we were to identify and pinpoint its experiential geography, four elements would stand out: being in the present moment, aliveness, openness, and freedom. These elements, yet again, also happen to characterize the life of a hermit—who may be said to be constantly living in the mode of becoming.

Being in the present moment: The traveler, by having to constantly meet new, strange situations, and by having to be intensely focused in order to process his ev-

Being in the present moment: A covered Muslim woman engrossed in prayer. Shiraz, Iran.

er-changing circumstances, tends to be more mindful than he is in his regular life. Being more fully immersed in the present moment is, of course, not exclusive to travel. It has been an ideal of many religious and philosophical traditions. It has been a central part of Buddhist, Hindu, and Christian meditative practices for millennia, and it has been given many different names, such as mindfulness or awareness. More recently, it has been discussed in depth by Eckhart Tolle, who called it "the power of now."[21] The ideal is to be in the now regardless of what one does — even during the most repetitive and boring activities. What is unique with travel, however, is that unlike all meditative, yogic, or spiritual practices, it *forces* one to be in the present moment. The new, the surprising, the alien, make the traveler become so absorbed in whatever he sees and experiences that he cannot help but be in the present moment quite often, and for considerable stretches of time. Paradoxically, mindfulness may be considered a kind of side effect of travel, since this is not something one consciously strives to achieve, but something that comes about effortlessly by virtue of traveling — it is inherent in the travel mode of being.

However, it is not that one is constantly in meditative repose or continually feeling something special or having peak experiences. Being in the present moment is something quite ordinary. Every person experiences this, even if less often, in everyday life too. For example, when one concentrates on important work or creates something meaningful, which absorbs him completely, or when one is captivated by a piece of art or music, he is fully present in the now. In rarer and

---

21 Eckart Tolle (1948-). His book *The Power of Now* explores the various aspects of being in the present moment.

A female Buddhist monk. Yangoon, Burma.

more extraordinary situations, such as a natural catastrophe, war, or other immediate danger, this experience is even more pronounced. When someone must fight
for his life, or exert overwhelming effort under time pressure, he exists wholly in
the present moment. In such situations, we often say that time stops because it
seems that the person has exited the normal experience of the flow of time. Probably, the common and crucial element in all of the above instances of being in the
present moment is *self-forgetfulness.* The traveler, immersed with all his senses, all
his attention in the new worlds he encounters, tends, more often than not, to become self-forgetful and absolutely focused in whatever he does or experiences.

Aliveness: A corollary to being in the present moment is the sensation of being truly alive. There seems to be a proportional relation between living in the
present moment and the aliveness one feels. It is as if life itself becomes magni-
fied, attenuated. When people become consumed by this spirit of aliveness, they
sometimes say "I feel so alive today!" The traveler tends to be in this state more
often than usual. It is not that he is necessarily joyous or in some rapture. On the
contrary! He might be immersed in something quite trivial or unpleasant, such as
negotiating the price of a kilo of mangoes with an Indian fruit-seller in Madras,
or having an embroiled argument with a hotel manager who overcharged him in
Hanoi. Both of these seemingly ordinary and common incidents require extreme
concentration because they happen in a foreign land—the rules and customs of
which the traveler is constantly in the process of learning and adapting to. Irrespective of the context of the situation, or the content of his experiences, he is forced to
react with focus and a sense of purpose to everything that appears in his path.

Openness: A traveler remains constantly open to the new. This mode of being continually open to whatever life throws at you is something quite different from what most people experience in sedentary life. In travel, one expects to be surprised as a matter of course. **[The Merchant & the Musician]** By lowering his defenses and putting in brackets everything he knows or to which he is accustomed, the traveler begins to see the world with fresh eyes, curiosity, enthusiasm, and a never-ending questioning of everything that is baffling or mysterious. Related to this openness is a greater willingness to change one's way of thinking, long-held views, and even things he considers to be certainties. This uncompromising and all-encompassing stance towards change is something that grows with time. Gradually, the traveler comes to terms with the realization that Heraclitus's maxim that "all is change" (or "everything is in constant flow") is probably the only constant and unchangeable truth in the universe.

Freedom: This is the primary element. Unlike normal sedentary life, travel life is permanently embedded in freedom. One is free to do as one pleases—stay in a place or move on; interact with a foreign culture or not; study, plan, sleep, or simply remain idle. This sense of absolute freedom is something that we all had when we were children and then lost at some point. As children, we had endless time to discover, play, and wonder. This childlike and playful freedom is reignited by travel and becomes the basic ingredient of life on the move. No one is waiting for the traveler. He does not have to be anywhere; there are neither work appointments nor project deadlines. Of course, this newly discovered freedom in travel must be checked and channeled if it is to bear fruit. It is to this aspect that we must now turn.

Freedom and Discipline

> *The creative act is entirely free or spontaneous, but the created effect is subject to the law of necessity. The creative act may be quite consciously chosen, yet the necessity invoked may be only imperfectly understood. In this case, I find that I have willed more than I knew, and thus face compulsive necessity in the environment that I have creatively produced. As a result, further willing is conditioned by this necessity. Hence, the created projection resists me. I must conform to its conditions, though I was its source.*
>
> —Franklin Merrell-Wolff

Travel is the paragon of Freedom. Few other human activities pertain to freedom as much as travel does. Vagabonding—itinerary-free and unplanned travel—may even be considered the freest of all human activities. The traveler is not bound by the shackles of everyday worldly concerns, a repetitive routine, the inescapable daily chores, and the need of social interactions that eat away one's time. Unlike someone living a regular life immersed in work, family, and friends, he is free to

The Merchant and the Musician

Vienna, Austria

I WALK IN CENTRAL CAIRO, along a crowded sidewalk. A street merchant approaches and tries to sell me a leather belt. I shake my head that I'm not interested and increase my pace. He follows me and persists. I walk even faster, eventually leaving him behind.

I walk in central Vienna, through Stephansplatz towards the Kunsthistorisches Museum. Amidst the urban noise, I suddenly hear the sound of a cello. I turn to my left and see a young man in full concert attire, cello between his legs, bow in hand, playing a suite by Bach in front of the Cartier shop. Unconsciously, I decrease my pace and come to a standstill.

Soon more people gather around him – an impromptu audience of random passersby. The piece finishes, everyone applauds. I find a corner and sit on the pavement – the museum can wait. The square has become an open-air concert hall. The cellist continues to perform. A magical spell is cast over Stephansplatz that echoes throughout Vienna.

The merchant increases the speed of the city. The musician slows it down.

The merchant intensifies the urban stress, the noise, the chaos. The musician makes you slow down, find your center. This holds true in all cities and countries.

Of course, we must accept the fact that the two are interdependent. That there would never have been a musician without the merchant. And that the merchant is an indispensable component at the heart of every city – with its many shopping streets, bazaars, and markets. We may even go so far as to suggest that, historically, all cities evolved out of an original small nucleus of merchants and traders who had come together to exchange goods.

I respect the merchant.

Yet, I vote for the musician. I always stop and listen.

conceive and construct his own daily program and his whole life as he sees fit. [Zurkhane] The only constraints to his freedom are those imposed by the world as it is and the laws of nature.

The essential element of his freedom is none other than Time itself. The traveler has almost infinite time at his disposal, which he may use as he sees fit. Yet this seemingly great blessing of endless free time can easily turn into the greatest curse. Just as it is not easy for a writer to face a blank sheet of paper that he must fill with his ideas or stories, a traveler's facing of "empty time" is equally daunting. The possibilities are endless; the potential paths, itineraries, courses of action are limitless; the activities (or inactivity!) into which he may choose to immerse himself are as diverse as the whole of life itself. Free time has the tendency to drag one along at its unceasing pace. Instead of becoming the work horse to which one may hitch a tool to create something he has in mind, free time often acts more like an untamed horse. To harness it, one must leave the field of freedom and seek assistance in what seems to be its exact opposite: discipline. Free time becomes effective and productive when it is prudently and purposefully channeled by means of

Cai Rang floating market, Vietnam.

discipline into a planned course of action. Thus, the traveler has to dance between his absolute freedom and the discipline necessary to harness it.

Every itinerary the traveler creates has its source in freedom. However, once the itinerary is created, many of the traveler's movements cease to be free and are governed by a formed freedom, a conscious self-limiting action. The apparent constraints imposed by oneself on one's freedom are, paradoxically, part of freedom itself—the freedom to limit the endless possibilities into finite actualities according to one's free will. However, once the creative act of free will has determined its self-imposed limitations, one has to follow the "law of necessity" and "face compulsive necessity" in the environment one has creatively produced, as Merrell-Wolff says.[22] All difficulties in one's journey, but also in one's life, can subsequently be considered as self-selected. Everything in the outside world that supposedly resists us may be seen as being in great part the result of our own choices. For example, if we freely decide to climb a steep mountain, we will be choosing to conform to its conditions, which are associated with the physical reality of a steep mountain. We will therefore have a challenging job. The mountain will apparently be resisting our efforts—and our freedom—yet this resistance was already prede-

---

22 The quotation from Merrell-Wolff (1887-1985) at the beginning of the chapter is from "Aphorism 36" of *The Philosophy of Consciousness without an Object*. Although the aphorism refers to the creative projection of the universe (or of man's universe) out of the Great Void, here the idea is used to shed light on something more ordinary and practical: the way we freely take any decision, but then have to conform to the conditions inherent in our decision (even if we "imperfectly understood" them). Merrell-Wolff's aphorism is applicable not only within his system of metaphysics, but to all human actions of free will. It explains how a big part of the struggles and difficulties in the life of man are actually self-chosen or self-imposed.

Zurkhane

Shiraz, Iran

IT IS ALMOST A FULL MOON. The bazaar domes cast their shadows on the labyrinthine alleys of the old town. We wander around with our new English-speaking Persian friends who lead the way. After a while, we approach an unassuming door that leads into a narrow corridor. "This is the oldest Zurkhane in town," one of our friends whispers, as if to suggest that we have just entered holy ground. "You know what Zurkhane means?" he continued. "The House of Power!"

A primal stench of sweat attacks our senses, mixed with a strange rhythmic drumming. Suddenly, at the end of the corridor, a huge domed room appears in front of us. In its center there is a large, sunken hexagonal area in which a group of men of all ages perform synchronized exercises. The men are barefoot, wear simple T-shirts, and have a short cloth wrapped around their loins. They hold fat wooden clubs, chains, and other objects that resemble medieval torture instruments. Perched in an elevated small box there is a musician, the morshed, beating the drum and chanting. By adjusting his tempo, he controls the men's movements. His chants, we soon learn, are passages from the great Persian poets – Hafez, Rumi, Ferdowsi. Awestruck, we sit quietly on the benches lining the wall and observe. We have been abruptly moved into another time and age.

The masterful drumming and singing of the morshed guides and reflects with such harmony the movements of the exercising bodies, while the athletes' graceful rhythmic pulses of muscle turns and twists are conversing so effortlessly with him that I feel as if the music and poetry are the bearer of some primeval spirit of power that is being transformed into raw human flesh with each stroke of the drum, right in front of our very eyes. It is as if the eternal spirit of the cosmos is just completing its final descent into the depths of matter and is being transformed into the power-full human body, exuding sweat and stench and bodily fluids. I suddenly realize that the real House of Power is not the building in which we are situated, but the body of man. *Each one of the athletes' bodies is a Zurkhane!* The house, or rather the Temple of Power, is the human body, which tirelessly expresses energy, strength, and power with each one of its movements. It is the athletes' rhythmic movements that like heartthrobs feed the inanimate building with Power. And it is the morshed's rhythmic chant that expresses this magical and mysterious flow of Power from the cosmos into the human body and back into the cosmos again.

In no other place, at no other instant in my travels or in my life in general, had I experienced with such clarity and purity the power that moves man. And though myself a weakling, rarely, if ever, having given to my body its due attention and respect, on this night in Shiraz, in the Temple of the Power, I kneeled and bowed in front of the unique movements and rhythm that the human body manifested. I felt that the Body took its rightful place next to Spirit and formally announced its equal power to rule and govern, control and guide the movements of our lives. For the first time in my life, I experienced with the strength of revelation that behind all my searches and travails in life there is and has always been *this same* power of the Body that silently – and almost invisible to me – sustained all of my movements. In the strange basement, with the graceful human bodies moving in unison with the mysterious and magical chants, I realized the simplest, yet one of the most important truths in life:

Body is Power. And I am a body.

termined in the original decision to climb the mountain. We knew that a steep mountain would be difficult to climb. However, we may not have anticipated the level of difficulty; we may have imperfectly understood how *truly* difficult it was. We all freely choose or create our life situations every day out of a set of options. Yet these situations, in turn, have to conform to laws, because everything created and residing in the universe is subject to laws.

Absolute freedom exists in a world outside of our own. Human freedom is always relative and moves within the limits imposed on it by natural law, space, time, and society. Our life, in a way, ends up being the interplay of our Freedom and *our freedom to restrain our Freedom*. Or, to put it another way, our life is the product of the dialogue between Freedom and the Discipline that Freedom freely chooses to impose on itself.

The harnessing of one's time through discipline, then, becomes one of the most important jobs of the traveler, and he ought to approach it with the same level of responsibility as a good worker approaches his job. By choosing his own constraints in a conscious and responsible manner, a traveler constantly lives with the maximum freedom possible and, at the same time, with the best and most pleasant limitations there are—which are those he chooses on his own and for himself. Through this continual play between free time and its harnessing, a traveler moves on, unencumbered by the heavy loads of sedentary life, and becomes one of the symbols of man's final liberation from all shackles and constraints.

CHAPTER IV

PARALLELS BETWEEN A TRAVEL-JOURNEY AND OUR LIFE'S-JOURNEY

*A*ll *problems of existence are essentially problems of Harmony.*
— Sri Aurobindo

The only really transitory aspects of life are the potentialities; but as soon as they are actualized, they are rendered realities at that very moment; they are saved and delivered into the past, wherein they are rescued and preserved from transitoriness... Man constantly makes his choice concerning the mass of present potentialities; which of these will be condemned to nonbeing and which will be actualized? Which choice will be made an actuality once and forever, an immortal "footprint in the sands of time"? At any moment, man must decide, for better or for worse, what will be the monument of his existence.
— Victor Frankl

Throughout the ages, people in many cultures have used the concept of a travel-journey as an allegory for life. Ever since Homer conceived of *The Odyssey*, our life's-journey has been related, talked about, and understood as having basic common elements with a travel-journey. The belief that our life has some aim and meaning, just as a journey has a destination and a specific quest, has inspired novelists, poets, philosophers, theologians, and recently, even psychologists.[23]

A long-term traveler cannot but relate the two and discover analogies and new ideas that shed light on both journeys. This chapter is an exploration of some of the parallels between the two journeys.

Potentialities and the One Life

At each moment of our lives, there are a million possibilities to choose from. We end up choosing just one; all the rest remain unrealized. With every decision we make, we instantly cause the collapse of all other possibilities. Every small, insignificant event in our lives, be it a delay of a few seconds to go somewhere or a chance encounter in the street, may at any moment change forever the course of our lives by destroying the bulk of the existing tree of possibilities. Our mind and will move in the domain of infinite potentialities. Yet, our life moves along a single path of actuality. Though we are permanently embedded in infinite potentialities, our life ends up becoming a single, one-dimensional, fixed, and unalterable historical trajectory that expresses a tiny part of who we are and what we could be. [**The Little Kingdoms**] There is a tragic element in the realization that, although we could choose one out of many different lives, in the end we are forced to choose only one. It is because of this that we may say that, in a sense, *all lives are tragic*. There is a constant tension between, on the one hand, our mental world that resides and moves in the universe of possibilities and is governed by the feeling of free will, and on the other hand, Life itself, which forces upon us an inescapable single life in a real universe of space and time, restraint and limitation. This tragic conflict is even more pronounced—and can be experienced as a strong existential angst—in people who consciously converse with the potential lives lying ahead of them. We could express the inner struggle of a person who converses with his potential lives as follows:

> I feel that the single life I must choose will impoverish me! I experience the collapse of all the potentialities inherent at each moment of my life as the dying of a part of me. For in these potentialities there is to be found a

---

23 A characteristic contemporary book by a Jungian analyst, James Hollis (1936-), has the elaborate title *On This Journey We Call Our Life: Living the Questions*, emphasizing the *questions* rather than the *answers*, as discussed in Chapter III.

The blue town of Chefchaouen, Morocco.

thousand loves, a thousand possible lives I can imagine myself living with equal satisfaction. My many interests, my many possible lives, are palpable. I'm in constant contact with them—they are my friends. How can I kill all these great possibilities lying ahead of me?

We could liken this inner dialogue to that of a chess player who laments the moment he makes his move for all the other equally interesting ones he could have made, each leading to a completely different game altogether. Just like every chess move, every one of our life decisions is made on the sacrificial altar of all the rest that forever remain unrealized. It is this *sacrificial element* of choosing one single life-path that makes deciding on the important matters of life so difficult. Choosing our life has no relationship whatsoever with the everyday choices we are engaged in. When we choose one menu item or one color of shoes over another, we are always free to cancel our order or change our mind. We may choose to make another choice.

Choosing *within life* includes its own power to cancel itself: "I choose to change my choice," "I choose to re-choose," "I choose not to be told to choose!" In the case of our *life taken as a whole,* however, none of these options apply. From the instant we decide on the course our whole life will take, the previous tree of possibilities collapses forever and a new one takes its place. Unlike with ordinary choices, there is no background that remains unaltered after the decision concerning the course our whole life will take. There is no going back. If we decide to watch a movie at a movie theatre, we may still decide to watch another movie later on. The substratum, the background of choices, is still there after every movie we

Higher Perfection

Nice, France

ENJOYING A 10-COURSE MEAL at one of the best restaurants in town. The atmosphere is great, the décor stylishly classic, the service impeccable.

Each course comes with an elaborate little ceremony: The maître d', with inconspicuous nods and a discreet sign language, like a maestro conducting an orchestra, leads a group of four to five servers. One server brings the proper cutlery for each course, another one brings our dishes each covered with a shiny silver cloche on a trolley, and after a cue from the maestro, the plates are placed on the table. When everything is finally in place, the maestro gives the final nod. With elegant movements that are similar to the simultaneous bowing of two orchestral violins, two servers remove the metal domes, uncovering the plates, while a third one explains the contents of the dish, all under the watchful eye of the maestro. There is an unspeakable harmony in all of this. Although the overall feeling is of something majestic, the delicate care with which they pamper us and the genuine love for their profession exudes intimacy.

Everything is running smoothly and each dish is better than the previous one. At the fifth course, however, something strange happens: At the uncovering of the plates, a vertical decorative carrot tower on my plate is knocked down by the cloche and falls flat on the plate. Nothing important, of course, since I will have to ruin the carrot tower myself in a few seconds to eat it. But this is not how our servers see it! It immediately becomes obvious that, according to them, this should not have happened and it is, well, an unacceptable aberration. The elaborate food décor is supposed to be first admired visually for a good 20 to 30 seconds and then, rather regretfully, it has to be destroyed by the patron in order for the food to be eaten. The diner has to first feast on it with his eyes and *then* eat it. Now, the little tower has fallen as a result of its unveiling, and the to-be-admired work of art, which was laboriously created by the chef and his team in the kitchen, has been compromised.

The flaw in the decoration of the plate has to be dealt with swiftly and decisively. The maestro suddenly loses his smile, and with a stern glance orders the poor server who had knocked down the carrot to raise it again, assisted by a colleague. They use a spoon and a fork to make it stand, but the carrot, as if struggling to remain the center of attention for few seconds longer before it departs forever from this earth, keeps falling! A third server joins in, and finally, the maestro himself. Within seconds, I have six to eight hands in my plate, performing all sorts of acrobatics with utensils and vegetables in front of my eyes. After about half a minute, the maestro feels that the stress created by the whole situation is having a more negative effect than the tragedy of the fallen carrot itself. I also sense that he feels we are entering the dangerous zone of the food getting cold. Just at the right moment, he makes a value judgment of immense significance: Operation Carrot Tower must come to an end. He orders them to stop trying to raise it, and apologizes for the incident with a witty remark that makes both of us laugh and the servers smile. A server then proceeds to explain the contents of the dish, and when he finishes, the maestro apologizes a second time for the fallen carrot *and* for the failed operation for its restoration!

All is well. Or rather *better* than before the carrot had fallen. I suddenly realize that this supposed little flaw and the attempt at correcting it was not a flaw. Rather, it was something that had taken the overall experience of fine dining service to a higher level. The flaw was handled with such amazing perfection that instead of spoiling the experience, it actually made it even more extraordinary. For without the carrot falling, we would never have witnessed the maestro with his orchestra performing under a challenging situation. It was because of the little crisis that the whole team was forced to use all its training, knowledge, and skills in order to raise its craft to the highest level possible. The service was so perfect that it was completely conscious even of its own minor imperfection. In the end, this *seeming* imperfection became the path leading to a *higher* perfection.

It seems that, of all things that lead to perfection, none is more crucial or decisive than the way we incorporate adversity into whatever we are striving to achieve. Perfection is reached, not by denying imperfection, but by striving to incorporate it harmoniously into any circumstance of our life. Every imperfection then becomes a springboard that raises our endeavor to an even fuller harmony. Seen this way, we may thus say with a renewed force:

Imperfection leads to a higher perfection.

watch. But if we have been studying medicine for two years and decide we want to change our studies, this will not alter the fact that we are two years older, or the fact that our study of medicine will permanently influence our life, forever carved as a "footprint in the sands of time"—as Victor Frankl says. The new set of possibilities ahead is another set, which covertly encloses the two years of our having taken a "wrong path." We cannot *cancel* our major decisions in life; we cannot go back in time. Similarily, we cannot alter a mistake we have already made, even though we can still strive to incorporate it harmoniously into our life. **[Higher Perfection]** Moving as we do in the unidirectional, unidimensional world of time, even not to choose—that is, to remain idle and not commit oneself to anything— is in itself a decision.

How then does someone who is in constant contact and dialogue with his potential lives, someone who loves a great number of possible life-paths, go about choosing a single life? Is it possible, even though one's life will end up being a one-dimensional path, to preserve elements in this path from the many other unrealized potential paths? And if this is possible, *how* can one preserve the substance, the soul, the main elements of these potential paths within one's single life-path?

It turns out that there are unexpected correlations between a travel-journey and our life's-journey, and that these, when carefully studied and meditated upon, shed light on both journeys and help us answer these questions.

Our Life's-Journey as a Wise-Line

Choosing a life-path is similar to choosing a travel-path. The problem of creating a path that would allow one to experience a representative cross section of a country is almost identical to the problem of creating a life *that would preserve the essence of the other main potential lives one must sacrifice.* We can think of our

The Little Kingdoms

Everywhere

WHEREVER I GO, there they are: the little kingdoms! The kingdom of the passport controller, the hotel receptionist, the train wagon attendant. Little kingdoms with powerful kings.

The kingdom of the passport-controller-king (a whole three square meters in size) has its own laws and rigid language, plus a never-ending line of human subjects showing reverence and humility to his royalty. The kingdom of the head receptionist (six square meters) with rules carved in stone is governed by a queen served by a beehive of workers and drones. She is usually stern, self-aware of her importance, occasionally granting precious audience to her subjects. The kingdom of the train wagon attendant always has a czar — in Russia it is the almighty *provodnitsa*. She governs a whole wagon as it travels through the Urals to Mongolia, and decides what time her subjects should go to bed, wake up, eat, or have fun, while punishing whoever challenges her authority with instant decapitation!

The list is endless. Men and women who have been assigned a small area of authority are to be found everywhere and they can pop up even in the most unexpected corners of the world. You may choose to be their obedient subject or consider your interaction with them as being a part of an innocent game. You may also choose to confront them, even occasionally fight them. But one thing is certain: You can never ignore them.

Within their little kingdoms, these people feel all-important, and occasionally omnipotent. They create and impose their own or others' rules. Above all, they demand respect. It is so funny to see how people manage to acquire an attitude of royalty once they have been assigned a little kingdom. How they love to have subjects to rule and how they enjoy giving orders. How they also need to be needed for their services.

I can see all the civil servants who suddenly become busy the moment you approach their desk, or slow down the moment a queue forms in front of them, as if to force you to respect their "difficult and tiring job" or simply make you plead for their attention. I recall the security wardens in the airports, the shopping malls, the offices, who use their formal language and implement the standard procedures, as if rehearsing some police academy exam. It is amusing to observe how they sometimes enjoy explaining the reason behind the troubles they are causing you, as if they are revealing a secret they were not supposed to share, so that you, the ignorant, may not even for a second dare think they are being irrational.

In a long journey, it is unavoidable that occasionally you may end up challenging the little authority of these big men or women. Sometimes you may have to confront or even have a duel to the death with such a king or queen. In these cases, just have your arsenal ready: know the subject matter well, have clear points and arguments, and if necessary, remember that there are always stronger kings or queens nearby that you may bring into the war, and with proper diplomacy, or showing of power, end up making them your allies so that you may win the battle. Above an impolite or bad receptionist, there's a hotel manager; next to the kingdom of the passport controller is the kingdom of the police; and near the security warden, there's always the company director.

But when all is said and done, maybe the best course of action in most cases where a king in his little kingdom goes too far is to simply study and observe him in order to learn something new about the specific kingdom and human nature itself.

Warriors in full regalia. Goroka Show, Mt. Hagen, Papua New Guinea.

life's-journey as being the equivalent of the wise-line in a travel-journey: *Our life's-journey is a cross section of the main themes of our life.* These main themes can be viewed as lying upon a surface, similar to the way the attractions of a country are scattered upon a surface. Our aim is to connect them in the most harmonious way possible. The concept of the wise-line of a travel-journey then becomes a great tool for understanding the totality of our life, as well as a guiding model in helping us create our life-path itself.

Earlier we discussed the concept of the wise-line (Chapter III). We saw that it aspires to represent the best possible cross section of the totality of a country and that its aim is to capture the soul of that country. We also saw that its construction was determined by four elements: the *magnification* of exploration, *isolating the common characteristics* of the country, *honoring one's loves and interests,* and allowing *openness to surprise* to modify it into something that is alive, constantly adapting and changing. We may now use these concepts from the travel-journey to shed light upon our life's-journey.

Creating Our Life's-Path: The Four Elements

Magnification

The magnification of *a theme in our life* may be thought of as being the depth with which we decide to commit ourselves to the pursuance of a specific goal. We may love birds, but we need not become ornithologists or workers in a bird park. We may just be willing to read books about birds, become bird-watchers, or maybe even just own a parrot. Similarly, we may love chess, but we might not be willing to play in chess tournaments or strive to become masters. We may just read chess books, study great historic games, and join the local chess club.

Every interest, every passion we have in life has a tag attached to it: It is the *level of commitment*, the amount of time and energy we are prepared to devote to it. Since we have limited time, means, and energy, we must share each of our loves with all of our other loves. This inescapable sharing determines the extent and role each of our loves takes in our lives. In a sense, these many loves and interests correspond to the infinite potentialities inherent in our lives: We could at any moment decide to work in a bird park and be with birds all day; we could decide to become professional chess players and play chess or write chess books for the rest of our lives. We have the freedom to change course and redefine ourselves whenever we want. But we cannot *be* a hundred people at the same time.

The way out of this universal human predicament of having to choose a single life out of the many we would love to lead is the realization that there *is* a way to live these other potential lives. Just as it is unnecessary to visit every single sight or attraction a country has to offer, it is not necessary to live to the fullest every possible life we could possibly lead. Rather, we may decide to keep many of our loves, and thus our potential lives, by incorporating them into our single path *in different magnifications*. We may decide to become a businessman, but still play chess at the local chess club, keep a parrot or two as pets, and visit bird parks every time we travel. Relating the idea of magnification in a travel-journey to the totality of our life's-journey, we may say that the degree of magnification with which we explore a country is the equivalent of the *degree of involvement* with each of our potential lives. By being engaged with these potentialities (although they are not part of the main path of our lives), we actually somehow still realize them to some degree. By not becoming a bird curator, yet loving birds and observing them, one retains one's potential life in the world of birds. One has simply incorporated it in one's life, albeit with a lower magnification. Just as by playing chess regularly at the club, one may be said to *be* a chess player too.

Isolating the Common Characteristics and Honoring One's Loves

Let us now examine the second and third elements of the creation of the wise-line in travel and see how they may shed light upon the general path of our life's-journey. Earlier we saw that one need not traverse every corner of a country, but need only identify the common characteristics of each region or cultural group, and wisely choose which representative parts to explore. The example of Peru was given, with its three different geographical zones (p. 68). The essence or soul of Peru can be captured in one's travels, not by seeing all of Peru or residing there for years, but by carving a single travel-path, a wise-line, through those representa-

Farmer returning home from the fields. Xijiang Village, China.

tive areas that incorporate many of its defining features. These representative parts then ought to be sufficient to give the traveler a good idea of the character of the whole region.

Similarly, and connecting this idea with our life's-journey, we can see that the possible lives we may lead have a value that lies not so much in their complete actualization in reality, but in the character, the overall substance of their nature. It is not so much the potential life in all its details that is the carrier of its true value and significance. Each potential life has general and universal features that are its true substance. There is a substance in chess that goes beyond actually playing chess. This substance can be found in its central ideas and principles. Chess is an art, a science, and a sport. By preserving the main elements that make chess so exciting, one may be said to be incorporating the substance of chess in one's life. A retained love of chess as an art, a science, and a sport preserves those parts of its substance that may teach us about life in general.

Whereas the idea of magnification helps us to see that each theme, each potential life of ours, can be incorporated in our actual life at different magnifications, this second element of preserving the substance of each life allows us to see the possibility that our potential lives can always coexist with all the others *at any point in time*. It is impossible to lead three lives simultaneously: be a chess player, a world-traveler, and a writer. Yet one may actually do all three at the same time by bringing together some of their principal elements and preserving their substance in one's single life-path. So, a writer may give examples from chess, and use chess to shed light on life itself, while at the same time be writing a book inspired by his travels (in this case, travel would be said to exist in the background as the source

Through the Others' Eyes

Papua New Guinea and India

HERE I WAS, in this remote part of the world called Papua New Guinea, being stared at by kids who considered me *the strangest sight*, since I was the first white man they had ever set eyes upon. For some, I was a ghost or a scary spirit from another dimension. One or two started crying out of fear I would eat them — for as it seems, just as my grandmother sometimes used to tell me the *black* boogeyman would come to eat me if I misbehaved, their grandmother had told them the *white* boogeyman was coming. It soon became obvious that I was much more of a curiosity for them than they were for me. Although I was there to see and study them, I was simultaneously being watched and studied by them a thousandfold.

Similarly, while exploring the depths of the central Deccan plateau in India, we passed through a remote village where travelers rarely, if ever, visit. We needed directions and lowered the taxi's car window, calling out to some local kids. In spite of the pouring rain, they ran up to the car, peeked through the window, and, to their utter shock, saw the otherworldly visitors. Wonder filled their eyes as they stared penetratingly at us and examined our faces. They stood in the rain mesmerized, dumbfounded. For a brief moment, I felt I was the ancient Greek god Hermes, descending from Mt. Olympus to bring a divine message to humanity, and that these kids were the chosen ones, having the privilege of a first contact. A shiver went through me as I realized that while I was searching for the gods of India, I myself was probably viewed as one by these kids ready to embrace the miraculous in their lives!

It is through poignant experiences like this that I slowly came to realize that *I am constantly being observed by the people I observe in a similar manner*.

The *"similar manner"* was the new breakthrough: I am a visitor in the world of peoples I encounter, but simultaneously they are also visitors in my world. I carry with me not just my personal features, mannerisms, and interests, but also the general way I think and understand the world. As a product of the society that nourished me, I am a living expression of thousands of years of European history and cultural development. I see the world and its people in a very specific — or should I say limited — way. Each person I encounter explores my world, as much as he can, in exactly the same manner that I explore his. Furthermore, he also tries to understand how I view him through the filters of my world. In this way, he may be said to be struggling to see himself through my own eyes. He asks himself, "How does this foreigner find my culture and manners? Who am I as seen from the outside, through this other person's eyes?!" I am a mirror into which every culture I encounter sees itself as an other. Each person who stares into my eyes sees not only me, but the reflection of himself in my eyes.

This reflection is the expression of the reciprocal relationship with the world I explore. Just as the world is *offered* gratuitously to me as a gift to be cherished and enjoyed, I simultaneously *offer* myself to the world as I travel. While enjoying the world and its cultures, at the same time, I myself am "enjoyed." While the world unfolds in front of me to be explored and studied, I am unfolding in front of everybody I come in contact with, and I am being explored and studied.

My world, the world I carry about as I move, is neither passive, nor neutral, nor leaves those whom it touches unaffected. At every point in my journey, there is an intersection where my world touches the newly discovered world; at this intersection there is a give and a take. I take something from the world I visit, but I also give something to it. I am transformed, but I transform it too. Most of the time these interactions happen naturally, unconsciously,

Observing the observers. Deccan Plateau, India.

without any premeditation. My world may be said to be "entering" the world I visit, just as the latter enters my world. My interactions with the village kids in Papua and India, for example, may have planted the seed of desire in one single curious child to travel outside his country—such indirect and hidden influences may end up marking the life of people in enormous ways. In the few photographs where locals had asked me to pose with them, and which are now scattered around the world in photo albums, the intersection of the two worlds is vividly captured and preserved forever.

But my influence is not just concentrated on the point of contact. I do not passively move around a stationary, immobile world in which I carve a path as a metal rod scratching a hard surface. Rather, I see my path as something similar to that of a sailboat's gliding on the water's surface. The line it carves slowly disperses, and in a wave-motion expands through numberless ripples across the whole ocean, with no visible end in sight.

It then becomes evident that while I travel, I do not simply exist *in* the world, but I also exist *for* the world. This has a significant influence on the world-traveler's mindset: If I exist for myself alone, I am free to do anything I like, with little regard to the effects I may have on the people I encounter. But if I also exist *for* the world, then my freedom is constrained—albeit in a positive way. I am free to be myself, yet I do not represent myself alone. I represent my culture, my people, and even the rest of the world that I have encountered thus far—to the extent to which the world at large has affected my character and thought.

The world-traveler, being aware of the world he takes with him wherever he goes, feels thus more responsible in his actions than a casual visitor. He is an ambassador of his people, his culture, his civilization, as well as an itinerant world citizen furthering universal understanding. And just as a local will do his utmost to make the best impression to the foreign guest, the world-traveler has to be a good ambassador of the world he represents and constantly carries with him. Knowing that he influences and transforms as much as he is being influenced and changed, his journey becomes *a responsible journey*. Suddenly, without ever having planned it, everything he does becomes part of an ambassadorial mission—a mission he has to fulfill with care, responsibility, and a sense of duty.

Traditional bread maker. Kuqa, Western China.

from which his writing springs forth).[24] Through preserving *the substance* of his other two potential lives, the writer may be said to live all three; he may be said to be at once a writer, a chess player, and a traveler. By allowing these apparently sacrificed lives (chess and travel) to simultaneously coexist in this way alongside and *within* his present life, the writer preserves them *qua substance* in the single life-path he follows.

We may thus make the generalization that if we manage to incorporate the substance of our loves in the single life we lead, we do not sacrifice our other potential lives. This is the way to honor one's many loves and passions in one's single life's-journey. It is to the extent to which *the substance* of these other lives becomes the body and soul of our one life that our life becomes more complete and in harmony with the core of our being. We may therefore finally have an ideal to which we may aspire: to preserve the substance of our potential lives in our single life's-journey. It is this that holds one of the keys to the fullness of our life, or rather, to our self-fulfillment.

Being Open to Surprise

Finally, we come to the last element that determines the wise-line: being open to surprise. In our travel-journey we allow the spontaneous and unpredictable an

---

24 It is more than obvious that the writer referred to here is no other than myself! The example concerning the mutual coexistence of the traveler, the chess player, and the writer *all at the same time* is personal, as was the example of the three themes—birds, chess, travel—used earlier under the subheading "Magnification." The latter three themes were constantly part of my life at various periods, albeit each being present at a different magnification.

Changing the donkey's "tire" at a traditional garage. Kuqa, Western China.

important role in forming our travel-path and molding it in a way that is not always in accord with our preplanned itinerary. In the same way, we should allow all the unexpected elements of life to mold our life's-journey.

Being open to surprise is not simply accepting that "life is change." It is the acknowledgment of the *possibility* of change and then the *mindful embracing* of it. Just as in our travel-journey we might be closed to the signs and contributions of the endless unexpected elements crossing our travel-path, we may similarly be resistant to change in our life's-journey. Consciously or unconsciously, we may be living in a castle behind fortified walls, fending off all suggestions from Life itself for change. We ought to first recognize the intimations of change when they arise, then mindfully embrace the fact of change, and finally, willingly change our course. Being open to surprise is being open to the fact that our life's-path is flexible and full of potentialities that may materialize at any moment. Even if the past cannot be altered, the future is still open, and anything is possible.

We have now reached the most important element of the parallels between a travel-journey and our life's-journey. We have seen that capturing the soul of a country may be considered the ultimate aim of a traveler. Let us now see how we can relate this to the ultimate aim of our life itself.

Capturing the Soul of Life

In a travel-journey, we defined the wise-line as the best route a traveler can follow on the surface of the Earth in order to see the most representative elements of a country. We then proposed viewing our potential lives (i.e., the main themes of our life) as similarly lying upon a surface. We then saw how our life's-journey can be seen as being a single wise-line connecting these possible lives—just as in a travel-journey the wise-line purposefully and harmoniously connects the various attractions, regions, and cultures of a country in such a way as to become a representative cross section of the country. Finally, we examined how the four elements that determine the creation of the wise-line in travel shed light on the subject of choosing our path in life from the many potential ones. We concluded by suggesting that our life's-journey is more self-fulfilling to the extent to which it preserves the substance of our other possible lives. Let us now take the analogies to their consummation.

In travel, the surface upon which the traveler carves his wise-line is the actual surface of the Earth. The wise-line ends up being his actual travel-path in the countries he explores. When it comes to our life's-journey, what is the "surface" upon which our potential lives lie? A train of thought suggests itself: As has been established, the wise-line in a travel-journey connects the most characteristic elements of a country, thus becoming a line carved on the *surface of a country*. Since we have related this wise-line to the way it connects the themes of our potential *lives* in our life's-journey, this surface cannot but be *the surface of Life itself!*

What do we mean by "the surface of Life"? This is another term for the totality of Life as experienced by a human being. Just as a traveler is out to explore a country, a human being can be seen as being here to "explore Life" through his body, mind, and activities—in other words, to live Life! If the ultimate aim of a travel-journey is to capture the soul of a country by carving a wise-line on its surface, we may propose (continuing the analogy) that the ultimate aim of our life's-journey is to *capture the soul of Life itself* by carving a wise-line through the themes of our potential lives.

But what do we mean by the "soul of Life"? This is not some palpable independent entity. Just as we spoke about capturing the soul of a country as an experience that cannot be described in words, we can similarly only speak in vague, general terms about the soul of Life. One aspect of capturing this soul is finding meaning in one's life. However, "capturing the soul of Life" is not just another term for finding meaning, as this would exclude a great segment of humanity for whom meaning has not become central in life. Rather, "capturing the soul of Life" refers to something more all-encompassing and fundamental:

Every human being on the planet, just as every plant and animal, fulfills a specific function by virtue of being alive. Each organism is a unique expression (out of myriad possibilities) of this principle and reality of Life, just as every atom or elementary particle is an expression of the principle and reality of the Matter and Energy in the cosmos. Each life-path of every living being is a unique expression of Life that has never before appeared in the universe in precisely that specific manner. With man, this unique expression has reached another level, because man has consciousness and self-consciousness. So, man's capturing of the soul of Life may become a conscious, purposeful endeavor that stands above the mechanical and biological forces of Nature. When viewed this way, man's capturing of the soul of Life falls into a category of its own. For man assigns himself high ideals, aims, purposes, and tasks to accomplish in life, and evaluates himself by his own highest standards. Unlike a plant or an animal, for which all is arranged by nature itself, man must struggle to express his unique qualities and potentialities in the cosmos in the most harmonious way possible. We may then assert that, just as a travel-journey is successful at capturing the soul of a country when it is well-planned and executed with a sense of direction and purpose along a truly *wise* wise-line, a human life conscious of its central themes—and striving for their synthesis—*succeeds in capturing the soul of Life by turning itself into a meaningful and harmonious expression of its many potentialities.*

The capturing of the soul of Life is not to be taken for granted. It is the result of struggle and mindful effort. As a traveler might fail to capture the soul of a country, man might fail to capture the soul of Life when he fails to harmoniously express his many potentialities in the single path of his life. Man's struggle to express himself is never-ending; it is part of what separates him from the rest of the animal kingdom. Man ceaselessly strives to harmoniously achieve his unique cross section of the "surface of Life," which is equivalent to the traveler's unique connecting-of-the-dots on the surface of a country. When he is successful in this endeavor, man's capturing of the soul of Life becomes a unique expression of the mystery and meaning of Life as it shines through his particular life's-journey. The harmonious connecting-of-the-dots of his life's many themes becomes his distinctive "footprint in the sands of time"—to recite Viktor Frankl's quote at the beginning of the chapter—by which he connects in a unique way to the Universal Life and its Great Mystery, both of which may be said to be infinite and beyond his grasp.

CHAPTER V
WORLD CITIZEN

"*I'm a citizen of the world (cosmo-politan),*" replied Diogenes,[25] the ancient Greek philosopher, to the person who asked him where he came from. This is the first recorded instance of someone identifying himself *primarily* as a global citizen, rather than as a citizen of one's city-state or in terms of nationality.

A few centuries later, the Roman Stoics would explore the matter in more depth. Influenced by the first globalized culture of the Roman Empire, Seneca[26] wrote the following in "On Leisure":

---

25 Diogenes (404-323 BCE), who lived "like a dog" (hence the Cynic school of philosophy that is derived from him—κύων, cyon = dog) in an urn in Athens, is mostly remembered for famously ridiculing Alexander the Great by telling him to move aside because he was blocking the sun, when the king had asked him if he could help him in any way.

26 Seneca (4 BCE-65 CE), the most influential Roman Stoic philosopher, bequeathed humanity a great oeuvre of practical philosophy.

*Students enjoy
a carefree moment,
drumming on
a pot on the way
home from school.
Upolu, Samoa.*

Let us grasp the idea that there are two communities—the one, a vast and truly common state, which embraces gods and men alike, in which we look neither to this corner of the earth nor to that, but measure the bounds of our citizenship by the path of the sun; the other, the one to which we have been assigned by the accident of birth. This will be the community of the Athenians or the Carthaginians, or of any other city that belongs, not to all, but to some particular race of men. Some yield service to both communities at the same time; some only to the lesser, some only to the greater.

A century after Seneca, Hierocles, another Stoic, introduced the important idea of concentric circles. He wrote:

For the first, indeed, and most proximate circle is that which every one describes about his own mind as a center, in which circle the body, and whatever is assumed for the sake of the body, are contained. The second from this, and which is at a greater distance from the center, but contains the first circle, is that in which parents, brothers, wife, and children are arranged. The third circle from the center is that which contains uncles and aunts, grandfathers and grandmothers, and the children of brothers and sisters. After this is the circle which includes the remaining relatives. Next to this is that which contains the common people, then that which contains those of the same tribe, afterwards that which contains the citizens; and then two other circles follow, one being the circle of those that dwell in the vicinity of the city, and the other, of those of the same province. But the outermost and greatest circle, and which contains all the other circles, is that of the whole human race. These things being thus considered, it is the province of him who strives to conduct himself properly in each of these connections to collect, in a certain respect, the circles, as it were, to one center...

As you can see, Hierocles uses a commonsense, geometric description that is self-evident and to which we can easily relate, if not instantly adopt. He then goes on to suggest that we make the circles of his scheme contract, bringing humanity nearer to us and making everybody more like our family.

These ideas were generally forgotten until modern times. The only person who dealt with the subject in any way was the German philosopher Immanuel Kant, but the idea of the world (or global) citizen truly resurfaced in the twentieth century. We saw the creation of the first global organizations, such as Amnesty International, Oxfam, Greenpeace, and, above all, the United Nations. Furthermore, after millennia of conflicts and wars, the majority of which were rooted in Europe, it only took the European nations 50 years or so after the end of World War II to become a Union. Actually, the current 70-year-long period of peace in Europe—the longest in its modern history—may be said to be ushering in a new Pax Europeana.

Apart from the global efforts of organizations and states, there have also been extraordinary efforts by individuals acting alone, such as Garry Davis,[27] who created the first official World Citizenship status. Davis singlehandedly issued his own world passports and campaigned like a modern-day Don Quixote against the existence of national states, which he considered the greatest evil of humanity.

At the end of the twentieth century, there has also been a revitalization of academic discussions on world citizenship as a political, cultural, or philosophical concept. Perhaps the most important publication that set the agenda for all subsequent discussions is Martha Nussbaum's 1994 article "Patriotism and Cosmopolitanism." Taking the Stoics as her inspiration, especially Hierocles's idea of the concentric circles, Nussbaum suggests a radical change in the United States' national education policy (implicitly, the rest of the world should also follow), one that would give predominance to the cosmopolitan rather than the nationalistic ideal. In the same article, she also offers four important arguments (the first two come from the Stoics) "for making the world citizenship, rather than national citizenship, education's central focus":

1. Through cosmopolitan education, we learn more about ourselves.
2. We make headway solving problems that require international cooperation.

---

27 Garry Davis (1921–2013) is famous for having stormed a session of the United Nations General Assembly in November 1948, proclaiming that "We, the People, want the peace which only a world government can give; the sovereign states you represent divide us and lead us to the abyss of total war."

Washing saris on the ghats of the Narmada River. Maheshwar, India.

3. We recognize moral obligations to the rest of the world that are real, and that otherwise would go unrecognized.

4. We make a consistent and coherent argument based on distinctions we are really prepared to defend.[28]

It is interesting that the once seemingly crazy idea of Diogenes, and the quixotic efforts of Garry Davis, are slowly finding their way into the academic articles of some of the world's most respected professors. However, the arguments in favor of world citizenship, and of viewing oneself primarily through the prism of one's humanity rather than one's nationality, go well beyond the practical concerns of lessening conflicts and furthering the understanding between nations. **[The Thin Film of Separation]** As we will go on to examine, the arguments have much stronger roots in our very evolution, in our human psychology, in our history, and much more. Furthermore, the idea of world citizenship is neither a new invention nor an ideal lying in the future. It is ingrained in our very nature as humans. It is time that all non-utilitarian arguments in favor of world citizenship be brought to light.

The "arguments" that follow are not, however, arguments in the conventional sense. They are as much a description of what already is and has always been the case in our human world. World citizenship forms the invisible thread that permeates our humanity, but since we do not see it, we deem it necessary to support it with "arguments." What follows, therefore, is not a set of arguments, but rather *a shedding of light* on some of the most important elements that make us human,

---

28 This addresses the respect due to one's nation, without according it a special status.

Evening Hindu ritual on the Yarmuna River. Vrindavan, India.

elements that happen to already include the primacy of world citizenship in their very foundation. Let us begin with the evolution of human societies.

Human Evolution

When we examine the evolution of human societies over thousands of years, we see that prehistoric man lived in a family or a small clan (a group of families). Gradually, these clans came together to create small villages. With the onset of the first agricultural societies and the creation of complex civic social structures, we moved on to city-states. Then we had the concept of countries, and then the all-encompassing empires. There has been a natural social evolution from the family to larger groups (reminding us of Hierocles's circles). This has to do with our social evolution as a species. But in historical times, things had also been moving in the same direction.

History

We must never forget that the modern, predominantly nationalistic state is a very recent phenomenon in the history of mankind. It is true that in some corners of the ancient world, nationality may have been important for some period of time. But the truth is that even then, most of the world's population lived in ethnically mixed societies—the Persian Empire, the Egyptian Kingdom, Imperial China. For the past two millennia, most people continued to live in such ethnically mixed conglomerations, be it the Byzantine, Ottoman, or Holy Roman empires, China or India. Furthermore, in this long period of human history during which there were

The Thin Film of Separation

Though you seek in garments the freedom of privacy
you may find in them a harness and a chain.
Would that you could meet the sun and the wind with more of your skin
and less of your garment.
For the breath of life is in the sunlight and the hand of life is in the wind.
— Kahlil Gibran

Ternate, Indonesia

"NO TOILET PAPER. USE WATER!" said my new friend Aan. "And only left hand, not right!" he continued. It was the first time someone had told me to use my right hand when eating, and my left when cleaning my bottom. I found it both strange and funny. However, later on, after actually applying it, I came to enjoy using my hands for these two distinct activities. I started relating to my excrements for the first time since I was a child. I began to explore them, discovering their many variations in tactile sensation and texture. There was also a newly felt sensation of cleanliness that only running water can bring – not toilet paper. Finally, I came to see in the simplicity of the act a kind of perennial wisdom. There seemed to be a connection to both the natural state of man and the child within us. Since eating and excreting are the most basic biological functions, what more natural to connect them with the most important part of our body – our two hands.

There's *a thin film of separation* between our hand and our anus when we use toilet paper. We introduce something between one part of our body and another. The same holds true for when we eat, using metal knives and forks or wooden chopsticks to introduce some distance between ourselves and the food, although in the end we will devour and assimilate it into our own bodies. Something similar happens with our relationship with the earth. In most human societies, we have long ceased to touch the soil. The bare soles of our feet do not make contact with the ground anymore, although they were constructed, through millions of years of human evolution, to do exactly that. Similarly, when we sit on a chair we do not have a natural distance from the earth; we create an artificial one, where our bottom is a half-meter above the ground. We may go further and meditate on our clothes – the thin film that separates our skin from the sun and the wind, as Kahlil Gibran says.

Just as in many Islamic countries they do not use toilet paper, in many other countries around the world they do not use utensils, but eat with their bare hands. In others, they prefer to walk barefoot rather than wear shoes, or they prefer to sit on the floor rather than on chairs. In many tribal societies, people are simply naked.

Modern man has created many wedges of separation that mediate his contact with the world for many reasons, whether it be a societal idea of cleanliness, an invented rule of propriety, or a newly acquired sense of comfort. He has substituted much of the natural simplicity of his life with complex and elaborate systems of social contact and behavior, many of which are unnecessary. It is an important moment when one realizes that these films of separation are neither universal nor compulsory and binding.

There is a new sense of liberation, a feeling of naturalness and of uncontrived movement, in eating with one's right hand, in cleaning one's bare bottom with the left hand, in sitting on the floor, in walking or swimming naked. There is no distance between our body and the actual things with which we come in contact. Our sense of touch becomes liberated and *alive* once again. Our skin becomes more sensitive and perceptive to the infinite variety of tactile sensations that surround it. A new universe of feeling the world around us opens up. The meat and vegetables we eat with knife and fork, apart from taste and smell, have a texture and other gifts for our senses. When holding a piece of lettuce in our hand, we come to feel its unique structure, its ruffled texture, its volume as a three-dimensional object. When gnawing on a bone of meat, we become aware of the fact that we are consuming an animal that was killed especially for us, and that we are carnivores. Food then ceases to be an object of taste that is solely related to the mouth. We come to rediscover with our hands a world we had left behind at a very young age.

Dispensing with some or all of these films of separation is one of the most liberating and *defining* acts of a world traveler. It is through these seemingly small and insignificant things, such as dispensing with the toilet paper altogether for the rest of one's life, or feeling free to eat with one's bare hands in front of others, that a world traveler becomes worthy of the title of world citizen.

no nation states, the unifying power was not nationality, but ethics and religion (Byzantium), or ideology and civic infrastructure (Imperial China), or simply the ideas and civilization of a grand empire (British Empire).

In the past two centuries, we saw an apparent step back, with the collapse of many such conglomerations and the emergence of nation-states—a development that has led to many catastrophic wars. Yet since the end of World War II, there has been a movement towards the formation of grander units, such as the European Union, the Union of South American Nations, and the Asia-Pacific Economic Cooperation Forum.

The seemingly contrary movement from empires to states in the past two centuries can now be seen in a new light: The previous empires were artificial and often forced entities—the result of conquest and assimilation. However, today's entities, such as the European Union, are the result of the voluntary desire of the member-states. The difference is important: The uniting force is now the result of the will of the people, rather than the power of a transient empire. The contemporary trend towards unification is thus healthier and seems more sustainable. We may envision a time when a French or a German will give primary allegiance to Europe rather than his own country. This is not now immediately obvious, and it might take decades for something like this to happen, but we can still imagine it.

Social Practice

An important fact that goes quite unnoticed is that, historically, societies seem to have *naturally* favored an allegiance to larger groups over smaller. The most ubiquitous example is when someone leaves his family to join the army in order to defend his country. It is not for his family that the soldier is prepared to sacrifice his life, but for his nation—even if there is the underlying presupposition that in doing so, he indirectly protects his family too. And if he falls in battle, it is not only his family that honors him, but also the nation.

Since ancient times, when Spartans and Athenians put their differences aside and came together to fight the invading Persians, people considered it nobler to relinquish one's narrower allegiance in favor of the larger group. In modern times, during World War II, we also saw states that were previously in conflict come together to serve a common purpose. Great Britain, France, the United States, and the Soviet Union joined forces to fight Germany. This alliance was even more important than defending only one's own state.

To defend and fight for one's country is regarded as being more important than to care only for one's city; defending one's city is deemed more worthy than caring only for one's family members; sacrificing one's own life to save one's parents or children is regarded as being more noble than saving oneself. The larger the circle, the more we have honored it throughout history. The largest group we can conceive of is the human race. It seems natural to simply move on and embrace this last group, the highest in this ascending hierarchy. By seeing things this way, we are not being idealists or dreamers, but rather realists; we are simply acknowledging and affirming what has always been the rule ever since human societies began to form large social groups.

Psychology

Apart from the evolutionary movement of societies towards grander, more all-encompassing forms, there is a strong argument to be made for a parallel movement in the personal psychological development of man. According to Carl Jung, there are stages in life through which every person must pass. During the first part of life, a person's world is his family. During adolescence, a transitional period, the person prepares to leave the family and go out into the world. In the industrialized world, family and school help one prepare for this new stage; in tribal societies, rites of passage are arranged. Then, the person enters society and creates his own life. After becoming the person he was meant to become, according to Jung, man has to connect with the cosmos (or God) and place his life within the context of an even larger circle. This final step takes place during the last years of his life.

Within this scheme there is a natural movement towards ever-increasing circles of being, each one simultaneously including and expanding the previous one. Psychologically, man's life-journey is one of expansion, moving from one's small family center towards the more-encompassing circles (a reminder of Hierocles).
[Nothing is Missing]

Monument Valley, Utah, USA.

The Accident of Birth

There is something more fundamental than all of these arguments that goes beyond the practical benefits of a cosmopolitan outlook, beyond any political considerations of utility, and beyond ethics and religion. Let us now examine this important point, which is taken from Seneca, by quoting from Nussbaum's article one more time: "The accident of where one is born is just that, an accident; any human being might have been born in any nation." Let us meditate on this for a moment. What does it really say?

First, it says that our having acquired our nationality was *a fortuitous event.* It is so by virtue of the way things in fact "came to be," and not by natural or logical necessity. As such, there is a kind of philosophical contingency here in the sense that our own nationality could have been any one of the hundreds on our planet.

Second, exactly because our nationality is arbitrary, any feeling we might have of it being more special than others cannot correspond to *the truth.* This does not suggest that one must not love one's nation more than others—just as we would never expect a mother not to love her child more than others. It is important, however, to be conscious that one's natural love, or even belief in the specialness of one's nation, is as incidental and arbitrary as one's birth into that nation. It is one thing to love one's country as naturally as a mother loves her child; it is another to project onto one's country or nation *objective* special qualities that supposedly hold true outside this loving relationship. [The Best Country in the World]

The Best Country in the World

Santiago, Chile

I ASKED MY 40-YEAR-OLD Chilean taxi driver in Santiago what he thought of Argentina. He replied that he had never crossed the border to the neighboring country and never intended to! Perplexed, I asked him how that was possible, given Argentina is never further than a two-hour drive from almost any border point of long and narrow Chile. He responded with a sense of certainty and shocking confidence that I still recall: *"Why leave Chile? It's the most beautiful, the best country in the world!"* I could not believe my ears! The guy wouldn't cross the nearby border not only because he thought there was nothing of interest to see on the other side, but also because he was *absolutely* certain that all the blessings God bestowed upon the Earth simply happened to have fallen on Chile and none other than Chile! Actually, the number of Argentina's natural, cultural, and other beauties is greater than Chile's, not least because Argentina is a much larger and more diverse country. Yet the taxi driver will live the rest of his life thinking his own country is superior, while any passing visitor from the other side of the world will know better. What is even more astonishing is that he had never even crossed the Andes by car from Santiago in Chile to Mendoza in Argentina, a drive that happens to be one of the great scenic routes of South America – a simple truism independent of any opinion anybody might have about Argentina itself.

I would later discover, to my great surprise, that this attitude is actually quite widespread, and that many people in many different countries think that they live in the best country in the world. It was always enlightening to hear the rational arguments these people invented in order to support their already-formed ideas and prejudices. It never crosses their minds that they have been brainwashed by family or school into thinking that their country is the best. Nor do they consider that because they grew up adapting to the environmental and cultural specifics of their own country, they ended up turning these into the weights and measures of evaluating all other cultures. Nor does it occur to them that they came to love *those* specific elements in their culture that they themselves had acquired, and thus their love for their own culture is in great part another expression of self-love!

These people are not different from every mother in the world who thinks that her first-born is the most beautiful child on Earth. A moment's reflection, though, will suffice to conclude that, just as there cannot be a billion most beautiful children in the world, not all 260 or so countries and territories on the planet can simultaneously be the best.

If you don't believe me that *your* country is neither the most beautiful nor the best in the world, then visit France. And if you are French, stay put!

Shared Legacy

There seems to be a cultural-evolutionary law whereby all important human inventions, discoveries, and advances become over time the common property of all humanity. Greek philosophy and art, Roman law and engineering, Islamic and Buddhist ideas have been assimilated and absorbed over a gestation period of millennia by many other cultures outside of their places of origin. It is because of this

Aristotle Never Tasted a Potato

Athens, Greece

"THESE ARE THE BEST POTATOES in the world! *Greek* potatoes!" said the waiter with a proud grin. We were having a traditional Greek meal under the Acropolis when, looking carefully at the dishes on our table, I suddenly realized that very few of the ingredients we were enjoying originated in Europe. *Aristotle never tasted a potato!* Neither any corn, nor tomatoes, nor chili, nor pineapples, nor chocolate. All these things were to be discovered 2,000 years later in the Americas. Furthermore, the ancient Greeks had never seen a Chinese, nor knew of the existence of China. Actually, they did not know any part of Asia beyond India; neither did they know of the existence of the Americas and sub-Saharan Africa (apart from Ethiopia). They never saw the Pacific Ocean, nor knew the true sizes of the other oceans, such as the Atlantic or the Indian. Basically, they did not know four-fifths of the Earth!

In spite of their many discoveries in the fields of mathematics, astronomy, geography, and medicine, their knowledge was so basic compared to ours that we may safely claim that a high school kid in an advanced society today knows more about the world and our place in it than all the students of Socrates ever knew. Add to that the fact that a contemporary kid can fly to any corner of the world within a few hours, may observe other galaxies with a simple telescope, see the inside of a cell with a microscope, find the answer to almost any question on the internet, and it becomes clear that the educated people of the past knew only a very small fraction of what is today common knowledge.

This accumulated knowledge, along with the discoveries of all past travelers, is concentrated in every guidebook the traveler consults. Our effortless access to it makes us forget what an incredible, even miraculous achievement this is, and how privileged twenty-first-century man is. Actually, every well-educated person on the planet today would seem like a god to the ancients, and were he transported to the past, he would be adored as such.

Many doubt that human society has moved forward, that science and technology and the ubiquitous learning establishments in the world have made our modern society better than that of ancient Greece, Persia, or China. Some say that man has gained a lot when it comes to external comforts and superficial knowledge, but that he has somehow lost in wisdom, or even that he has lost his soul. Let us not enter this controversial and much-discussed subject. Let us do something else, much simpler, that may increase our feeling of gratefulness for living now, in this era: direct our attention to the simple daily pleasures we experience. Let us, each time we enjoy a selection of fruits from around the world, a strawberry tart or a cup of coffee, be mindful of the fact that none of these existed for our ancestors, and that the discovery of even one of them by the ancients would have sufficed to make them feel that they had discovered the ambrosia of the gods.

We tend to underestimate these little carnal pleasures of life, but let us never forget that the fifteenth-century Age of Discovery was the result of the passionate seeking of a faster and cheaper route to the Spice Islands. The irony is that the most sought-after of these spices, the craving for which may be said to have single-handedly changed the world, was the small inconspicuous clove—which nowadays is just one ordinary spice of many in our kitchen cupboard. Sometimes I have the feeling that if an ancient traveler from the East had brought a durian fruit to the ancient Persian court of Darius or the Athenian Agora, humanity wouldn't have waited 2,000 years for the Americas and the Pacific to be discovered!

Pelion, one of the many preserved medieval villages of the Maritime Alps, France.

that Nussbaum may call herself a Stoic, while a modern German might decide to define himself as a Buddhist.

Over a period of 5,000 years of human history and, before that, over the period of prehistory and human biological evolution, almost every place on this Earth has had its moment of great achievement, irrespective of how long it lasted. In addition, there are the natural wonders of the Earth that are randomly distributed in all continents, and each country can claim a few for which it may—unwarrantedly—feel pride in "owning." There is a sense in which every single country, even every single region or local group on the planet, has something unique to offer to the rest of humanity—even if that one thing happens to simply be its mere existence and difference from all the rest. There is something truly wondrous in the fact that every single place on the planet is unique, and that each group of people, be it a large one like the Han in China or a miniscule one like the Kwaio tribe in the Solomon Islands, has something valuable to give to the rest of humanity. Even if a nation has little to contribute to the world today, its ancestors may have had a larger impact at some point in the past, which we may discover if we look thousands of years back. We know who invented things quite recently in our history, but who was the first to invent the fishing hook or the hunting bow? Maybe it was someone 30,000 years ago in Sierra Leone (which is today miserably beset by civil wars), or an Eskimo surviving in the harsh cold of North America. Similarly, thousands of years ago there must have definitely been an imaginative Central American woman who had the inspiration to cook the strange-looking potato tuber for the first time—a staple food that ended up conquering the world. **[Aristotle Never Tasted a Potato]** In every corner of our planet, at some stage in man's long

Christian Orthodox monasteries situated on top of the Meteora mammoth rock formations, one of the natural wonders of Europe. Thessaly, Greece.

evolution, at least one great discovery or invention has been made that was subsequently adopted by the rest of humanity.

All these human contributions are part of *a legacy we all share*. In this sense, then, we can claim that every single person today is who he is as a result of the collective contributions of all other nations and of every region of the Earth.

Our Common Humanity

The moment the idea of a nation arises, inescapably it arises in dependence upon the existence of other nations. We may even say that national pride requires the existence of other nationalities in order to exist! If all human beings were French, the idea of "being French" would be meaningless. This is another example of the basic Buddhist axiom of interdependent origination referred to earlier—that everything arising in our world is dependent for its existence upon something other than itself and thus has no inherent separate self-existence.

But there is still an even deeper idea: Just as nationalities are interdependent on one another in order to subsist, *a world composed of nationalities* is dependent upon the idea of *a world without nationalities*. One may retort that the first is a reality (the current reality of our world) while the latter is simply an abstract idea, or an ideal towards which humanity one day may, or may not, move. However, this is not correct. The idea of a world without nationalities is already something we experience as a reality. It is a reality that goes unnoticed because it is the substratum we take for granted: The moment one speaks of one's nationality with respect to other nationalities, he indirectly presupposes a common quality upon which he

Universal Brotherhood

Amsterdam, Holland

I HAD JUST BROKEN every rule in the book: I drove the car the wrong way on a one-way street, then along a pedestrian brick-paved lane, entered a plaza full of people sitting around coffee tables, did a U-turn between the tables, then illegally entered another one-way street, and finally parked on a double yellow line facing the wrong direction! I noticed the bewildered stare of locals who, without doubt, had never before seen such an errant car – in this arche-typal city of bicycles. As always happens in such situations, not one but a group of Dutch policemen (who were busy giving other cars parking tickets) witnessed the last phase of my incredible feat. One of them approached the car and, after seeing my foreign license plates, gave me a big smile and said: "I see you come from far away!" We then started talking about my travels as well as my impressions of Amsterdam. After a couple of minutes of friendly and warm conversation, and before the policeman addressed the issue himself, I told him I knew that I was illegally parked, but that I was waiting for my friend to pick up our laundry, and that it wouldn't take long. He smiled and said, "No problem. Take your time, but don't stay here all day!" No ticket, no arguments, no stress. Not even a single reference to my several traffic vio-lations earlier. Just human understanding, a warm smile, connection, and caring.

During my journey, I tried to look beyond what appears on the surface of a human being, beyond the stereotypes associated with ethnicity, race, and occupation. I discovered that the overwhelming majority of people did the same thing with me: They first addressed me as a human being and then as anything else – in this case, a traffic offender.

There is an invisible connecting thread that goes through each one of us like a string through beaded pearls. Behind the masks, titles, and clothes we all wear, there's a naked human body with functions we all have in common. There's a human mind, emotions, and a human will that moves us. There are our common daily concerns, dreams, loves, and fears. By removing every surface mask, I feel I can communicate in depth with *every* human be-ing. The human stare, the smile, the gestures, in spite of their infinite variations and quirks, belong to the common library of our shared humanity – to which each and every one of us has access and can read and understand. Behind every mask, I can see myself: It is I who struggles; it is I who sees and speaks. Behind every mask is the real person.

But there is another, deeper level of connection: All these people now alive on Earth are *my* people, born and living in this specific day and age. Billions upon billions of people have appeared on this planet before me, and billions more are to be born. Yet at this unique inter-section of the present with eternal time, I share this world of mine in this specific historical moment with these particular humans. This is a connection that is even stronger than the reality of our common humanity. We all happen to be on this planet *now.* We all see the world, its history, and its future through the eyes and mind of twenty-first century man.

Yet there is still a third level of connection: *All* of us now alive will not be here 130 years from now.* Every person alive today, every person I come in contact with or observe from

---

* After writing this, I discovered that this idea is as ancient as history! Herodotus (*Histories 7, 46*) writes that Xerxes, after gloating at the view of his impressive army and fleet at Abydus in Asia Minor, suddenly and unex-pectedly wept. When his uncle Artabanus questioned him, Xerxes said that he had just realized that in 100 years, none of those soldiers would be alive!

afar, will die within the span of a few decades, give or take, from the date of my death. Here we are, all these pulsating, active, living creatures, having appeared on this planet through some unknown and mysterious convergence of circumstance, only to soon vanish again – like shooting stars carving a bright path along the dark infinite stillness of a seemingly indifferent universe. Every person I speak with, every person I see, every person whose path I cross, is on his deathbed! But I see that all of them are oblivious to this fact – they move about and act as if they will be here forever. Occasionally, I feel like standing on a makeshift platform and addressing all of the passersby. I feel like talking to them, like Seneca** once did, about the shortness of life, about how little time they still have left to see some of the beauties and wonders of their own home, and inciting them to stop running and being preoccupied with their little daily chores. I want to tell them to start traveling with the urgency of a person who has only a few more years left to live. And we all have only a few more years left to live.

Of these three human bonds connecting us all – the real person behind the mask, the uniqueness of our common existence *now*, and the invisible thread of our common destiny in death – the last is the most powerful and the one that acts as the strongest catalyst towards the appearance within us of an unadulterated feeling of Universal Brotherhood.

** Reference to Seneca's *On the Shortness of Life*.

makes comparisons. This quality is none other than the basic concept of a human being—the common humanity we all share. **[Universal Brotherhood]** It is as *human beings* that we are different. So, while we affirm the concept of nationalities and differentiation, we simultaneously affirm an underlying oneness. Our common humanity is neither a rationalization nor a deduction. *It is as much a given as our nationality.*

World Citizen

It is this common humanity that forms the basis for our status as natural-born world citizens, just as our differentiated characteristics are the basis of nationalities. But let not the nationalists or ultranationalists feel threatened! By affirming our status as world citizens, we are not inventing something new or adding any strange quality to what we already are. A world citizen does not deny nationality, that which makes each nation different. *He affirms it.* It is because of the incredible variety of human civilizations and cultures that our world is so fascinating and worth exploring. If the whole world were identical to our own home, there would be no reason to travel. The diversity of our world is its strongest, most defining characteristic. And this global diversity is possible only because of national identity. It is with respect to this background of nationalities that the world citizen defines himself as such. While he affirms his nationality, he sees it as belonging to something much vaster, more beautiful, more substantial and important: the

Nothing is Missing

Ha Long Bay, Vietnam

THE FIVE YOUNG German travelers sitting with me at the beach bar were full of questions. "How do you travel for so long? Don't you miss your family? Which is your favorite country?" On the one hand, I felt like a celebrity, and on the other, as if I were in a court being cross-examined. Fortunately, after a while all of their questions focused on travel advice, so the celebrity status prevailed.

As it turns out, the traveler is not the only one to ask questions. Quite often, he is also being questioned about himself, his country, his journey, even about his ideas, his philosophy, and how he views the countries he has visited or the country in which he happens to be traveling at the time. He has to "explain himself" and his actions. Occasionally, he even has to defend his life's choices, since long-term travel is seen by many as a kind of oddity, even an aberration from living a normal life.

Of all the questions and interrogations that the traveler must respond to, probably the most common are those related to his traveling on his own and whether or not he misses home. Friends and relatives are among those who repeatedly ask the traveler if he misses them. If we were to put all of these questions into one long condensed form, it would look something like this: "How can you enjoy traveling *on your own*? Don't you feel like *something is missing* when you *cannot share* these wonderful experiences with *the people you love*?"

Depending on the person who asked, I would answer differently each time, addressing what was most baffling to each one of them. Yet all my answers revolved around the same central ideas, each addressing one of the four emphasized parts in the questions above:

1. *The traveler is not alone.* Actually, he is almost *never* alone (unless he consciously chooses and *tries hard* to be on his own). He is almost always surrounded by people, be they locals, other travelers, or passersby. The overwhelming majority of the people he encounters are openhearted, kind, helpful, and friendly. The traveler, even though he may be considered a traveler-hermit to the extent that he is alone in his unveiling of the inner significance and meaning of his experiences, still is not alone in the sense of being away from people. Similarly, he is never lonely. He is so much immersed in the activities of the world that the feeling, or even the thought of loneliness, never arises. It is up to him to decide the level of socializing he wishes to have in any part of the world – the frequency and depth of his interactions. Finally, unlike what some non-travelers may think, there is rarely, if ever, any sense of alienation in being among people who speak a foreign language. One of the first things that a long-term traveler discovers is that human communication is largely nonverbal and that even in remote places in which people do not speak English, most of the basic and universal messages, such as "I'm happy," "I'm tired," "I'm hungry," can be understood by all people.

2. *How can there be something or someone missing from the present moment?!* When you are truly where you are (and not thinking of something else), then nothing is ever missing. If you divert your attention from where you are and start thinking of other people and asking, "How great would it be if this friend of mine could see this?" you cease to be fully immersed in the experience and become lost in your thoughts. The same thing happens when you get out of the moment and try to capture it by taking a photo or a video. At this moment, you begin to become more mindful of capturing the moment rather than being *mindlessly lost in it*, which is a synonym for being mindfully aware in the present moment.

3. *Sharing one's journey with those who are not present is impossible anyway.* Why be

Papete, a new friend in Papua New Guinea.

preoccupied with this? However, there are always people nearby with whom we *do* share our experiences by default. Wherever we happen to be, there are usually other people around us who are part of the common world we share by virtue of fate having brought us together at this exact place and time. When you enjoy the magical sunset at Mindil Beach in Darwin, Australia, after having explored the famous sprawling seaside stalls, there are hundreds of others enjoying it with you. These up-to-that-moment-unknown people are now part of your new world, and you may, if you so decide, get to know them better and even come to befriend or love them as your relationship grows. This brings us to the final and strongest of all points addressing the issue of loved ones, the next item on this list.

4. *The people you love are not a fixed, unalterable set!* We would dare say, they *should not* be a fixed set. Friendships are created through a conscious mutual effort that involves openness to the unknown person and a movement towards him. There was a moment in time when each of your current friends was not a friend. At some point, even your spouse was as unknown to you as every person you meet in your travels. Every friend you have ever had was as much a stranger to you as this old Papuan man you have just met, who sleeps in a thatched hut with his pig. Yet if you would start talking to him with openness and an earnest desire to come to know him, you would soon discover that not only is he an extraordinary person but that, in spite of your age difference, your different cultures and upbringing, you could become friends. Before you know it, you would realize that you have made a new friend, Papete. You would know that you will remain in the heart of one another for the rest of your lives, even if you never meet again.

By allowing the group of people whom we call "our loved ones" to continually expand, we realize that this group is actually limitless. It is only narrow-mindedness and a superficial convention that makes us divide people into friends and strangers. The world-traveler soon learns to see in every person he interacts with *a potential friend*. And as his relationship with some of these formerly unknown people deepens, he not only makes new friends in every corner of the world but also comes to realize that those he previously thought of as his unique friends back home are actually part of a never-ending ascending spiral of human connections.

Evening at one of the oldest continuously inhabited towns in Europe. Matera, Italy.

largest all-encompassing nation called humanity. Our nationality and our common humanity are intertwined in a mutual interrelation through which both are understood and defined.

Seen in this way, there is no real conflict between nationalism and globalism. On the contrary: *It is to the extent that a nation becomes more global in its achievements that it becomes admirable.* The ancient Greek philosophers and mathematicians had fulfilled their national greatness the moment they had become universal. At that point, they ceased to belong to their nation only and ended up belonging to humanity at large. Similarly, the Islamic Golden Age, the Italian Renaissance, the French Enlightenment, and the British Industrial Revolution do not "belong" to the nations that created them but to all of mankind. Nobody "owns" the Enlightenment or modern technology.

What applies to the contributions of nations as a whole applies, even more so, to individuals—our great ancestors. Our ancestors' achievements have been bequeathed to humanity at large, not simply to the people who happen to have been born on the same spot centuries later! Believing that we own what was created in our homelands in the past is based on the naive assumption that, somehow, we have had an involvement in what our great ancestors created and, therefore, may take pride in those creations. In truth, our ancestors are judged on their own merits, as we should be. If we want to be worthy of our great ancestors, we ought to create analogous worthy deeds in today's world.

The greatest sons and daughters of every nation (for which, still unwarrantedly, each nation is proud) are those who have managed to fulfill their highest aim, and in achieving it, have become universal. The laws of nature that the English-

The mysterious massive moais lit by night. Easter Island, Chile.

man Isaac Newton discovered belong not to the person who discovered them (nor his nation), but to humanity as a whole. Plato's *Phaedo* is not Greek, but universal, as Shakespeare's *Hamlet* is not British, nor Beethoven's *Violin Concerto* German, nor Sri Aurobindo's *Savitri* Indian. *The culmination of every supreme nationalism is a consummate universalism.*

Through considering all the interconnections we have with other people, which are rooted in our human evolution, our history, our social practices, our psychology; through rationally examining the accident of birth, and how each and every place or nation has been indispensable in creating our present-day shared legacy; and, finally, through realizing that our nationality is the other face of our common humanity, we may gradually come to see ourselves as belonging to the most expanded and greatest circle of all: humanity itself. As such, each and every one of us already is, and always has been, a world citizen.

ADDENDA

Addendum I

PLANNING AN AROUND-THE-WORLD JOURNEY

A Few Initial Considerations

Once the big mental shift is achieved and the Earth is seen as a single travel desti-nation in its own right, we may begin to think about it in a new way. It would help, for example, to assume that we have an extraterrestrial guest whom we are obliged to show around the Earth. If the Earth were a single country and we were to ex-plore it in exactly the same way as we now go about exploring any country, would we not begin by searching for the Earth's highlights and then try to fit as many as possible in our travel itinerary? Can we speak about the highlights of the Earth just as we speak about the highlights of France? And how would we go about iden-tifying them? Even if we could identify these highlights, aren't all these lists sub-jective and meaningless?

Let us begin by dealing with this last question: The answer is *no*—these lists are not meaningless. There may be a part of the lists that purport to single out the highlights of a country or region that is truly subjective. Yet, we must not go to the other extreme and altogether deny that each country, each region of the Earth, has *objective* highlights—places one must definitely visit.

Just like everything else in life, not all places are created equal. And definitely not all regions of a country or the Earth are *worth* visiting. Athens is a sprawl-ing metropolis of four million people, but its important attractions, architectural beauty, historical monuments, and cultural life are all concentrated in the four square kilometers around the Acropolis. The rest of the city is an ugly repetition of the same apartment buildings, built in the 1960s and 1970s. Once you've seen a couple of these neighborhoods, you have seen them all. The same principle applies to most cities around the world, although the notable exceptions, such as Paris, London, Vienna, and New York, whose beauty extends well beyond their small historical center, must definitely be on any list of the Earth's highlights by virtue of their exceptionality!

The same reasoning may also be applied to whole regions of countries. As discussed earlier, great parts of the Earth are repetitive (e.g., the scenery of an ocean or that of the Amazon River), while other parts are simply uninteresting in terms of landscape or flora and fauna or human cultures. Having this analysis in mind, we may attempt the ambitious task of finding the highlights of a continent and then, subsequently, the highlights of the Earth for any world-traveler. Later on, we will be using Europe as an example of how one may go about working on this task.

We may break our list into three: 1) the *most important* highlights of the Earth, 2) the *very important*, and 3) the *important* ones. This is equivalent to categorizing the highlights as five-star, four-star, and three-star. Another way to consider the categories is to assume they correspond to a two-year around-the-world journey, a four-year one, and a six-year one—adding more highlights to each longer journey, in order of their importance. Of course, this is just schematic, since many five-star sites or wonders are randomly scattered around the globe, and many have to be missed in order to create a more balanced journey that will include more three- and four-star locales.

Of course, such a list will be insufficient *as a whole* to satisfy everyone. Depending on the character, interests, nationality, and age of any individual traveler, other highlights, regions, or whole countries would have to be included. Furthermore, every person *already* lives in a specific region (say, Europe), which he probably knows and understands better than the rest of the world. In some cases he *already* may have *traveled* to a number of places that he need not include in an around-the-world journey.[29] Still, creating a highlights list forms the main core around which each traveler may create his own personal list, by adding or subtracting countries or places.

When we discuss "highlights," we do not just discuss *places*. *Everything* on the Earth's surface, in the sea, and in the sky must be included, such as animals, plants, rivers, volcanic eruptions, tropical storms, and the varied activities of humans—such as ceremonies and fiestas, unique customs, food, and music. No visit to Bali is complete without attending a gamelan orchestra performance; no visit to China is complete unless one tastes many Chinese dishes; no visit to the rainforest counts as such unless one listens to the forest's sounds at night while actually sleeping in it; no visit to India is complete if one does not attend a Hindu funeral

---

29 For example, in my around-the-world journey I did not include the Near East, the United Kingdom, Scandinavia, or Eastern Europe, because I had already traveled there earlier in my life.

ceremony. Some of these events may be country-specific; others, such as trekking on an active volcano, may only be possible in a few places. In our highlights, we will include some of these activities, events, and happenings, even though we cannot exhaust their variety, nor easily compare them with one another.

The Five Axes

Let us boldly proceed then: How do we go about first choosing the "highlight countries" of the world? Our criteria must not be narrow—such as natural beauty or historical importance alone. They must encompass the totality of the elements that make up a country. The best way to begin is by starting from the continents— the largest entities into which humanity has historically divided itself. We may then ask a simple question: Which are the most *representative* countries of each continent? We will not necessarily be searching for the most beautiful in terms of natural beauty, or even the most important in terms of their present-day political status. We would rather be asking a *negative* question: What are those countries that if one *does not see*, he will end up lacking in his understanding or overall experience of the continent?

There are five axes around which one can build one's tentative highlights of a continent: geography, size, history, culture, and beauty. These axes may be considered as the context within which the traveler will base his analysis and understanding of countries. They are also the means whereby the relative merits and importance of each country or region will be evaluated. Just as an apprentice woodworker must understand the principles of wood carving and know the types of wood, so must an aspiring traveler study and learn his subject matter. The five axes we propose may be seen as the *principles* of *the craft of traveling*. They help organize one's thoughts and focus the attention on the most important elements, preventing the aspiring traveler from getting lost in the infinity of the world.

1. Geography

Geography is the most basic axis around which every journey is built. It encompasses not just the climatic zones (e.g., desert, rainforest) and the type of terrain (e.g., mountain, prairies) but also such aspects as the distances between places and the mode of travel. For example, Samoa, being a small island, will be explored by car; China, a huge country, must also include flights.

2. Size

Although pertaining to geography, size merits a category of its own. The size of a country is crucial in determining not only its relative value but also the time needed to explore it. In some sense, size belongs to all the other axes: It is a geographical feature, it determines the country's historical position and, to an extent, its cultural influence on the whole continent. Historically and often culturally, larger countries are generally more important than smaller ones. (Consider the significance of France as compared to Slovenia, or China versus Korea.) However, one must be careful not to take this too far. For example, Greece and England, despite their small size, have been more important historically than many larger countries in Europe.

Consideration of size becomes more important in Asia or America. The size element goes beyond history or culture. Even if one were to claim that Brazil's history is quite recent and lacks chronological depth, it must still remain the most important country of South America for any traveler because of its sheer size—it is almost half the size of the continent. One cannot easily skip the huge countries of the world—they have a way of staring you in the face!

3. History

History determines the depth of a country's past and gives value to many of its attractions. Countries like Italy, Greece, and Peru are huge, open-air archeological museums. In large part, these countries have significance by virtue of their important past, remnants of which have been preserved. Modern Cairo is interesting as a destination, but the nearby ancient pyramids of Giza may be said to be more important, and thus no visit to Egypt may be considered complete without seeing them.

4. Culture

Culture is the soul of a country's society. It is what gives a nation its character and identity and makes it unique. There are nations or countries that can be grouped together in terms of their common culture. Ethnicity and language are central here. The Arab countries pertain to the Arabic civilization, while almost all Latin American countries share a common Amerindo-Hispanic culture. One need not visit every Arab or Latin American country in order to experience the respective common culture. On the other hand, within some countries, such as China, Indonesia, or Papua New Guinea, one may find many diverse cultures. No thorough understanding of these countries is possible without some acquaintance with their cultural diversity. In China, there are at least 100 million indigenous people that belong to over 50 different linguistic and cultural groups. Indonesia and Papua New Guinea are modern artificial states that were created by forcefully uniting their many diverse nationalities and cultures. Reading about and becoming familiar with a few of the cultures that make up these countries is imperative.

5. Beauty

Beauty is the final and most controversial axis, because many people believe they belong to the best ethnic group or live in the best country or both (Capsule "The Best Country in the World"). There is a widely held belief that beauty is subjective. Yet the matter is not that simple, if for no other reason than that philosophers have been arguing about it for millennia. As the *Stanford Encyclopedia of Philosophy* says: "The nature of Beauty is one of the most enduring and controversial themes in Western philosophy, and is—with the nature of Art—one of the two fundamental issues in philosophical aesthetics."

A very general definition of beauty, taken from the *Oxford English Dictionary*, is: "Beauty is a characteristic of a person, animal, place, object, or idea that provides a perceptual experience of pleasure or satisfaction." As you can see, problems arise from the generality of almost any definition of beauty. Many philosophers (especially the ancients) have held beauty to be objective, but many modern philosophers stress that a subjective element must be introduced to balance the absolute position. There is some consensus towards a position that goes something like this: Although we cannot directly find a standard of beauty that sets out the qualities that a thing must possess in order to be beautiful, we can describe the qualities of a good art critic or a tasteful person. Then, *the long-run consensus* of such persons becomes the practical standard of taste and the means of justifying judgments about beauty.

Without wanting to delve deep into the Philosophy of Aesthetics, we must accept some universal standard of beauty, at least for those things that the overwhelming majority of the world would come to a consensus about. There are some natural wonders (which were named as such for a reason!) and landscapes that are awe-inspiring and may be said to be the embodiment of natural beauty. Examples of this are the Monument Valley in the United States, the Perito Moreno Glacier in Argentina, the Jiuzhaigou Valley in China, and Huahine in French Polynesia. These places arouse, in all who set eyes upon them, "a perceptual experience of pleasure or satisfaction" (definition above), which may be said to be objective.

Of course, we must still be careful when following this logic, because for a South Pacific resident, "wondrous" Huahine may seem ordinary and boring. Just as for someone living in the barren landscapes of Nevada and New Mexico, Monument Valley may simply be "another bunch of rocks"! There is an element of subjectivity here that is largely dependent on one's birthplace. The immediate surroundings of one's birthplace notwithstanding, we may consider these natural wonders or extended areas of extreme beauty to be our most secure and truly objective starting points.

What about human structures—the cities, villages, and otherwise human-modified lands of a country? Here, the subjective element becomes more pronounced. What constitutes a beautiful building or a beautiful garden depends on how people from various cultural backgrounds evaluate man-made beauty. Yet even here, all objectivity is not lost: For example, starting from the historical long-run consensus of humanity as a whole, we may claim, without fear or prejudice, that Paris is *indeed* one of the most beautiful cities in the world, and that chaotic, polluted, and tasteless Manila is one of the most ugly. And we can, with equal confidence, assert that the historical towns and the traditional villages of France, with their well-preserved stone houses and cobbled streets, definitely belong to another level of aesthetics than modern, all-concrete villages to be found in every country of the world. Similarly, the manicured human-cultivated vineyards and fields of Tuscany are much more beautiful than the desolate, ugly country-scapes usually enveloping large modern cities.

By having all this in mind, we may now begin to make a few general comparisons between countries. To illuminate the above reasoning and support the case for objective beauty, it might be helpful to use some rather extreme examples. Very few countries in the world condense as many natural wonders and awe-inspiring landscapes into so small a surface area as New Zealand. A country that boasts so many attractions *must* be classified as being among the most beautiful of the world. On the other hand, even if there is some beauty in the monotonous landscape of Moldova, broken only by even more monotonous Soviet-era towns full of identical apartment blocks, not a single person on the planet will claim that Moldova is more beautiful than New Zealand.

We may proceed further and argue that there is a self-evident and implicit aesthetic evaluation in the tour-operator's choice to include Vienna and Prague in tours of Central Europe while excluding Frankfurt or Stuttgart. This, when examined carefully, is actually the result not so much of the long-run consensus of the agencies that organize these trips but of the travelers' themselves. For it is the travelers, influenced by their perceptual experience of pleasure or satisfaction at seeing and walking around Vienna and Prague, that have actually spread the message (and photos) to all future travelers about the beauty of these places. Throughout the centuries, travelers have come to an unwritten consensus that these two cities are magnificent.

One must not take the "long-run consensus" idea too far, however, or one may miss many hidden jewels lying along his path. Nevertheless, the idea is important in the context of demonstrating that beauty has a crucial objective aspect that must be taken into account in both evaluating countries and in forming an itinerary.

Creating a Tentative Wise-Line for the Exploration of Europe: An Example

We are now ready to tackle the issue of identifying the highlights of a continent. We will use Europe, the most studied and visited of all continents, as an example of the method we'll be using and the way the previous ideas will be applied. The method we will follow can be broken down into three parts. First, we will identify the core countries of Europe by applying the method of the five axes. Next, we will add regions and cities to complete the list. Then, we will have a brief discussion about how we may take into consideration various cultural events or festivals. Finally, we will find a way to connect everything and form a travel itinerary.

A) The Core Countries of Europe

Using the Axes

Beginning from the first axis of *geography*, let us use the simple scheme of Norman Davies.[30] He divides Europe into four geographical zones: 1) the great European plain that begins at the Urals and the Caspian Sea and ends in the Loire Valley of France and the Atlantic; 2) the mountain spine that includes the Carpathians, the Alps, and the Central Massif of France (to which we may add the Pyrenees); 3) the Mediterranean lands, which basically include the south of Spain, most of Italy, the Balkan Peninsula, and Greece; and 4) the smaller Danube basin, which includes the southern part of Central Europe and part of the Balkans. However, for our purposes, we must add an important fifth region: Northern Europe, which may include the British Isles, Scandinavia, and the Baltic States. This is the broad geographical division of Europe, with its corresponding natural features, landscapes, flora, and fauna.

The first axis, *geography*, suggests that we include at least one country from each of these five major geographic zones of Europe. At first glance, France suggests itself as the best candidate, since it touches the great European plain, the Alps, and the Mediterranean. Stretching from the Alps to the Mediterranean, Italy also seems to fulfill a large part of the geographic criteria. Finally, Germany, which includes the Alps and the Danube basin, and lies at the heart of the continent in such a way that one must traverse it in order to move from one country to another.

The second axis is *size*. The largest countries of Europe are Russia (if we decide to include it in our European tour rather than saving it for Asia), France, Ukraine, Spain, Sweden, and Germany. Of course, Russia and Sweden may be big, but a large part of these countries is in frozen tundra with a monotonous landscape, inaccessible most of the year. If one decides to visit Scandinavia, the fact that Sweden is the largest country should play a role in one's decision. Similarly, visiting Russia rather than Ukraine is a prudent suggestion, not just because of size, but also because of the former's more important historical role.

The third and extremely important axis is *history*. Unlike places such as the Pacific Islands or New Zealand, history is a constituent part of the identity of Eu-

---

30 Norman Davies, *Europe: A History.*

rope. Many of the highlights of Europe are historical monuments (such as Delphi in Greece), ancient cities (such as Pompeii in Italy), medieval towns (such as Carcassonne in France), or even prehistoric sites (like Stonehenge in England). In almost every European country, the discerning traveler can see the historical process of the development of a country and feel its different layers. In Rome, for example, one may find buildings or structures from almost every century of the last 2,500 years!

Although all European countries took part in the formation of Europe's history, some countries have been more important and influential in actually shaping it. There are objective historical criteria that decide this. Nobody can deny that France has been much more important historically than Norway or Montenegro in determining the course of Europe. France's influence and legacy is easily seen in many parts of Europe today. Similarly, Italy has been much more important than Belgium or even Poland, not least because of its Roman past, but also because of the Italian Renaissance. When all of these historical factors are taken into account, we can easily come to the conclusion that some countries stand out in terms of their historical weight—Italy, Greece, France, and Germany are much more important historically than most others.

The fourth axis is *culture*. Slavic Russia, Belarus, and Ukraine have a common history, similar cultures, and speak more or less the same language. If one wants to explore the Slavic world of the former Soviet Union, one need only visit representative parts of this area, not all countries. Similarly, the Danes, Norwegians, and Swedes have more similarities than differences and are nearer to one another than they are to the Italians—in culture, social norms, and even temperament. The Central European countries of Germany, Austria, and Switzerland are again "close relatives"—not only do they speak German, but most of their customs originate from a common branch. All of these ethnic and cultural groupings must be taken into account when deciding on the highlights of Europe. One need not visit all German speaking lands, nor all the Slavic or Scandinavian countries, in order to experience the corresponding cultures. The main idea is to obtain a general understanding of each culture by exploring its common representative aspects. These cultural common characteristics are often shared across borders.

Let us now come to the final and, as discussed earlier, the most controversial axis: *beauty*. Historically, many have considered Italy to be the most beautiful country in Europe, as evidenced by the European Grand Tour.[31] Similarly, for centuries France has been considered one of the most captivating countries, not only because of its impressive natural beauty and well-preserved medieval villages but

---

[31] The Grand Tour was popular among Northern European aristocrats and upper-class men from 1600 to 1840. They visited the biggest attractions of Europe as part of an educational rite of passage. The Tour's final destination and highlight was Italy, where these men often stayed for a year, visiting important cultural and historical sites, mainly from antiquity and the Renaissance periods.

also because of its rural human-modified landscapes, such as its cultivated lands and gardens, which have set a high standard that many have followed.

The Alps and their surroundings also stand out for their beauty. As such, the south of Germany, western Austria, northern Italy, and Switzerland are strong candidates. The southern parts of the United Kingdom and Spain have also long been considered places of great beauty. Moreover, Greece has its unique islands scattered in the Mediterranean.

Identifying the Core Countries

We are now ready to tackle the task of forming the "highlight countries of Europe."[32] It becomes obvious that France and Italy immediately emerge as the two first choices for belonging to the core countries of Europe. France is the largest country in Europe. It has a very rich history dating from Roman times up to the twenty-first century, and its cultural influence in Europe has been unparalleled. It also has the most beautiful collection of medieval villages on the continent, or even the world. We may thus say that France is one of the countries that *defines* Europe.

Similarly, Italy is the quintessential European country because it connects all the threads of European history while also encompassing a great part of the continent's geographical diversity, beginning in the Alps and ending at the southernmost tip of the European peninsula. Italy is home to ancient Rome, Florence, Venice, Tuscany, and the Northern lakes; it holds the ruins of Pompeii, the mosaics of Ravenna, the Sistine Chapel. Germany also takes prominence, not just because of its size and its importance in the history of Europe, especially in the last centuries, but also because of its natural beauty, especially in the south. In terms of ethnicity, the German-speaking world is also the second largest after the Slavic group.

There are many countries in the north that are contenders for representing that part of Europe: the Scandinavian countries, the United Kingdom, Ireland, even Iceland or Greenland at the very top. If we are to choose only one, however, we can only seriously consider the United Kingdom. No other European country was more important in disseminating the European civilization throughout the globe. By employing only a few thousand people, Britain governed the world through the most organized civil service and sophisticated diplomacy ever known. Britain lent its language to the world, invented the concept of organized travel, most sports, the modern male suit and tie, and much more. It was the site of the Industrial Revolution—not to mention a colonial powerhouse, with an empire spanning North America, Australia, and New Zealand. One may claim that it single-handedly created most of the elements that constitute our modern world! Furthermore, al-

---

32 In the example here and later, when forming the travel itinerary, Russia and the other East Slavic countries are not considered as part of Europe. The only reason for this choice is to make the example simpler—since Russia extends all the way to Vladivostok at the far eastern end of Asia!

though it is a relatively small country and quite geographically homogenous, Britain's history has deep roots—with ancient megalithic structures like Stonehenge, Roman ruins such as Hadrian's fortifications in Scotland, and the Roman city of Bath, as well as an incredible collection of medieval historic villages and period buildings. Finally, Scotland and the south of England boast unique natural beauty.

These "big four" (France, Italy, Germany, and the United Kingdom) seem to be the core countries of Europe. Similarly, each continent has its defining core countries that the traveler must include, even if only a partial exploration of them is possible. The remaining choices depend on the traveler's taste, interests, and time available.

B) Completing the Highlights by Adding to the Core Countries

Let us now complete the list by examining which other areas of Europe must be included in the highlights. The European tour would not be complete without visiting parts of other countries, such as Spain, Switzerland, or a number of Slavic states. Spain has been important in shaping not just a big part of European history but also world history during the Age of Discovery. Subsequently, it also had a major influence on the Americas. We may proceed with the following reasoning: If we are not going to include the whole of Spain, then we ought to choose its most characteristic areas, which would include Madrid, Granada, Seville, and a few of the Pueblos Blancos in the south.

Historic and important cities must also be considered as attractions to be visited, even if one decides not to explore the countries in which they are situated. For example, one may visit Amsterdam, Vienna, or Prague without traveling around their respective countries. These three incredible historic capital cities are fascinating microcosms that enclose much of Europe's heritage. Likewise, Switzerland has beautiful historic towns like Zurich, Bern, and Lucerne, as well as trains that ride through the Alps, showcasing its impressive natural beauty. The Slavic countries of Slovenia and Serbia may be visited, as well as Sarajevo, if one wants to include a representative Muslim Balkan town. Part of Croatia, with its enchanting Dalmatian Coast and historic Dubrovnik, may be added. Budapest in Hungary is another option.

From the four major Scandinavian countries, one or two may be chosen, depending on one's time or interests. St. Petersburg, although part of Russia, is the most European of all Russian cities, and hence may be included in the European tour, especially if nearby Helsinki is added to the itinerary.

As a final step, a few natural wonders as well as regions of extreme physical beauty may be added separately if they do not already belong to the countries one will be visiting. One may include, as mentioned earlier, a train journey in Switzerland or a hike in the Austrian Alps. Visiting Greece to experience insular Mediterranean life and the natural wonder of Meteora could be the final brushstroke of a European tour.

A possible list of highlight countries and regions of Europe would then look something like this:

a.   Highlight Countries of Europe:
      France
      Italy
      Germany
      UK

b.   Other Important Regions:
      Part Spain
      Part Switzerland
      Part Serbia/Slovenia/Croatia (or some other West Slavic countries)
      Part Scandinavia
      Part Greece

c.   Highlight Towns and Natural Wonders:
      Amsterdam
      Vienna
      Prague
      Dubrovnik (and/or Sarajevo, Budapest)
      St. Petersburg (with Helsinki)
      Train ride through the Alps, Switzerland
      The Norwegian fjords
      Some Greek islands and Meteora

This example and analysis is given simply to indicate the *process* of thinking that may be followed as well as the *principles* and *general philosophy* that guide the formation of such a highlights list. It is not meant as a definitive proposal of the highlights of Europe. Although the four core countries are a foundation upon which an expanded itinerary will be built, the other selections contribute to the final itinerary and determine not only the final mix of countries that will be included, but also the actual travel route.

C) Adding Events

Together with exploring the important countries, the traveler must also try to delve deeper into each culture by attending various events during his travels.

A variety of events offer a view of living traditions that is characteristic of each place. The traveler can attend a mass in either a Catholic or a Protestant church, or both; attend a classical music concert in one of the great concert halls of the continent; coordinate his itinerary to be at specific places during the time of big festivals (such as the Oktoberfest in Munich, the Carnival in Venice, or the Orthodox Easter in Corfu). A visit to farmers' markets or fish markets in coastal villages is a great opportunity to see locals going about their regular routines. Events also include dining at a gourmet French restaurant with its elaborate dishes and service, touring the wineries of Spain, and visiting local food producers, such as olive-oil makers in Tuscany. Of course, recreation, such as cycling along scenic routes, whitewater rafting, or skiing in the Alps, also offer different angles into the various countries.

D) Deciding the Mode of Transport

The travel route and detailed itinerary must also include the modes of transport that will be used during different legs of the journey. Europe is best seen by car, although train and plane can be used to reach the remotest areas or to save time and money. The selected European core countries and their nearby neighboring partial countries may all be reached by train, bus, or car, while St. Petersburg and the Greek islands may best be reached by flights from the center of the continent. The modes of transport selected at different legs of the journey must also be based on the traveler's total travel time, budget, and travel preferences.

E) Creating a Tentative Wise-Line

Once the aspiring traveler has researched and selected his various destinations, he must then harmoniously connect the dots on the map in order to create his tentative travel route, identified earlier as the *wise-line*. What will finally be included in this first tentative travel route will be the result of a balancing act. This tentative travel route will be adjusted to accommodate travel times, event dates, and other unique circumstances. While constructing this travel route, the traveler must also be mindful of several other things:

- Choose the country's optimal points of entry and exit for the specific travel route.
- Avoid backtracking (going through the same region or town more than once, or doing a return journey along the same road).
- Avoid going through areas of similar natural, cultural, or architectural character.
- Save time by choosing the proper means of transport for each different leg of the journey.

- Allot enough time for the places that have more to offer.
- Exclude places the traveler has visited on previous trips.

A similar procedure and methodology can be followed to create the high-lights of the rest of the continents and, consequently, the whole planet. This methodology, rooted in the five axes of a continent, offers a solid framework to select countries and destinations in order to create a well-rounded and relevant travel itinerary. Implementing this methodology for South America, for example, one could choose Brazil, Argentina, Bolivia, and Peru as its core countries.

Addendum II

A GLIMPSE INTO THE ACTUAL DAYS
OF A WORLD-TRAVELER

The daily life of a world-traveler can be divided into five activities. Everything he does falls into one of the following categories:

(1) Travel
(2) Planning
(3) Study
(4) Errands
(5) Rest

Most days include more than one of the above activities. There is a modicum of planning almost every single day, as one has to arrange the next day's activities. Sometimes while one is at an attraction, one also reads about its significance and history from a guidebook or tourist brochure—all this is study, too. And, of course, the traveler might drop off his clothes at the laundromat on the way to an attraction, to be picked up in the late afternoon. He may also check his emails in the evening, or write a letter to a friend, or study more about a place he has visited or will visit. Thus, a number of these activities naturally occur more or less every day. How one organizes his journey, of course, depends on his idiosyncrasies and tastes. I found that gathering these activities into *whole days* was better for me. It allowed my travel days (the first and most important on the list) to be more pure and untainted by other activities, such as running errands or planning. So I ended up having travel days, planning days, study days, errands days, and rest days.

A travel day was for exploration, seeing new places, visiting sites, attending events, and interacting with people. An errands day was a day in which I stayed in one place in order to do my laundry (approximately once every three weeks), repair something (e.g., shoes, suitcase, camera), buy supplies (e.g., mosquito repellent or a flashlight), or do something special (e.g., find a specific book or go to the post office). Then, I would have planning days in order to plan the rest of the journey—usually at the end of the travels in a country or some extended region (say, the Deccan Plateau of India). Finally, every three or four days, I would stay put in one place and have a rest day or two. Sometimes I did not follow through with my scheduled rest days for one of many reasons, the main one being my having been carried away by the excitement of discovery. Under these circumstances, I would postpone my rest so that I could see more of the new place or delve deeper into the culture. If a week or more went by without a rest day, I would then take a longer resting period lasting three to four days. As a rule, self-imposed after my having experienced extreme cumulative fatigue a few times, I would take an entire week of rest after two months (nine weeks) of travel. This corresponds to six weeks a year of rest, which is what most working people in Europe get, when you include Christmas, Easter, and other public holidays. Sometimes I extended these rest weeks to a fortnight or three weeks by adding a study and planning week. This would happen after a long, uninterrupted period with no or very little rest, or when I needed time to plan the exploration of a huge country. In three or four instances, I extended my rest period in order to completely replan the rest of my journey (in light of newly gathered experiences and travel wisdom). For example, in New Zealand, I spent three weeks working on adding Central Asia and the Silk Road to my itinerary.

Let us now look in more detail at each of these five activities.

Travel

Travel is the main job of the world-traveler. Travel usually means motion and exploration. A travel day, most of the time, is a day of activity and movement. However, this does not cover the complete definition. Sometimes one may be said to have a travel day even when he stays in one place. He is immersed in some form of exploration even when he attends a ceremony or a concert or he stays at a place to simply observe a natural phenomenon or wildlife. One may be said to be in the mode of travel when all his senses and attention are focused on experiencing elements of the country.

Most of the travel activities may be divided into the three most typical modes in which they are to be found: *travel per se, attending events*, and *finding accommodation*. Although the last one may be put under daily errands or chores, there is a reason that it is included in travel, which will become clear later.

Travel per se is exploring the world—visiting places and interacting with the foreign cultures. We may, however, divide this into the three main ways of travel: on foot, by car (or bus, train, boat), and by plane. The greatest magnification of exploration becomes possible when actually *walking* in a town or a village; entering a museum, a home, or some other building; or hiking in a place of natural beauty.

But travel is not just traveling. It also includes experiencing elements of travel that cannot strictly be classified under the category of *travel per se* in the sense of "moving around." An important part of travel consists of *attending events*. Events are usually a condensed expression of many elements of a culture. A Latin American fiesta, for example, becomes a focal point of a whole region where most of the character and soul of the local culture may be experienced by the traveler with little effort and much fun! A grand fiesta, like the Brazilian Carnival in Olinda or Rio de Janeiro, condenses many traditions of the country, elements of its history, its music, the variety of its many local dishes, and much more.

Events, however, are not just fiestas. The word "event," as used here, has a very broad meaning. There are many other types of events that enrich one's travels, and the traveler ought to actively inquire about and search for them. There are the normal events of everyday life: a wedding, a party, a sports event, an ordinary funeral, Sunday mass at a church, or prayer in a mosque. These provide, yet again, a rich cross section of the culture, and occasionally, like weddings, they might be whole fiestas in their own right. To these normal events, we may add many others, such as attending a classical music concert in Vienna, a theatrical play in New York, a kabuki performance in Japan, or a Chinese troupe practicing with traditional instruments in a tea garden in the center of Chengdu. An event is also dining in a high-class restaurant in France or in a kaiseki restaurant in Japan, with their traditional elaborate service. Even enjoying street food in Bangkok can qualify as an event. Such events are entire microcosms that enclose within their apparent smallness a great many elements of a culture. A Japanese kaiseki meal is not just "dining out," just as attending a performance of Beethoven's Fifth Symphony is not simply "listening to music." Both of these events are two of the supreme achievements of the Japanese and German civilizations, respectively. There is history, art, culture, beauty, and much more in just one kaiseki meal, such that it may be said to encompass all the central elements of the Japanese soul. Similarly, Beethoven's Fifth is not just another piece of music.

Let us use the example of attending a concert performance of Beethoven's Fifth to examine more closely what it involves, in an effort to shed light on why and in what manner *attending events* is central to one's experience of a whole culture. When one ponders upon this incredible creation of the human spirit, one realizes that Beethoven's Fifth is not simply Beethoven's own creation. It encloses, even condenses within it, the whole of European civilization! First, it is one of the supreme expressions of polyphonic orchestral music. Second, it is the manifestation of the craftsmanship, the technology, the factories that created the very advanced instruments that the musicians play. Third, it is related to the architectural and acoustical design of the concert hall in which it is performed and the European tradition of creating special halls for different types of performances. Fourth, it illustrates a society's dedication to its musical tradition, with an educational system that fosters and cultivates learning in order to create such big orchestras. Fifth, there is the music lover who has cultivated his ear so as to appreciate this elaborate and complex composition, who by attending the concert sustains the high level of classical music performances. Finally, we may think of Beethoven himself; how he was both the product and the expression of a whole era, of a society that valued the *individual,* encouraging him to create anything he wished in a free-flowing manner.

It is an impoverished traveler indeed who concentrates more on "seeing" things and moving constantly from place to place without actively seeking such events in his journey, or sometimes even staying in one place for a few days so that he may come to experience a number of them.

Finally, there is one more type of event, which is perhaps the ultimate for a traveler: being invited by a local family to dine in their home or to attend a social event such as a wedding or a birthday party. Of all the events of a journey, none are more vivid and unforgettable than those few magical moments. (Unfortunately they are few, because you cannot always invite an invitation—although one has to be bold enough to suggest it when an opportunity arises!) It is the pinnacle of travel to enter the home of a Persian in Iran, a Mayan family in Guatemala, or a Tata Somba villager in Benin, in order to listen to the local language and observe the inner life and workings of the people *from within* the basic constituent unit of a culture, which is the family. One may have read a hundred books and seen a thousand photos of Tibetan nomads, but horseback riding for half a day to reach them and then staying in their yak tent for a few nights becomes an all-round, four-dimensional experience. Simple, everyday activities, such as sleeping on a makeshift mattress next to the herds' dried dung or listening to the nomads' bucolic songs while sharing their simple but tasty food, become *engraved* in one's soul forever. When the traveler later views the photos he took with the nomads, he will smell the inside of the tent, taste the food, hear the language and songs, and feel the tactile sensations of the floor. These memories will not be, like most memories, "faint copies of impressions."[33] They will be as *strong, alive, and real* as the actual impressions that gave birth to them. Such precious and rare encounters are little epiphanies and worth their active pursuit. It is at such events, usually towards the end of the exploration of a country, that one may spontaneously capture the soul of a nation.

The last, and more mundane of the three activities of travel, is the *search for accommodation.* It might seem strange to include this basic survival activity in

---

33 The definition of memories, according to the British philosopher David Hume (1711–1776).

"travel," yet it is not only an integral part of travel, but also happens almost every day. It is not possible for a long-term traveler to plan his accommodation in advance in the same way that other travelers do. He simply moves on and has to find a new place to stay every two to three days on average. The actual search for accommodation develops into some kind of technique that improves with time and experience. It may take anything from half an hour to two, or occasionally longer, to find the proper lodging that fits the personal tastes of the traveler. During this search, the traveler visits a number of different hotels or lodges in order to get a feel of the prices and quality of accommodation in the new place. He then chooses the best value-for-money accommodation and checks into his room. However, one may also combine this activity with seeing specific areas of a town or city that he visits during the process. Or, conversely, *while* exploring a town, he may also be searching for accommodation. Nowadays, with the internet and the many websites available for assisting travelers, as well as the feedback concerning accommodations from customer reviews, one may book a room blindly in a big city and be certain the room will be satisfactory. However, in the small towns and villages of most of the world, such easy access to information is not available. Furthermore, one is constantly on the move and cannot incessantly be connected to the internet, trying to create a personal short-list of accommodation options at the next stop. Most importantly, the traveler often cannot predict in advance where he will be at the end of the day, since being free to stay longer at a place he likes or to skip a place he does not is an integral part of long-term travel. In many instances, when the accommodation offered is unique, such as the riads in Morocco (renovated centuries-old historic Moorish mansions) or the delightful bed-and-breakfasts in the UK, the places that one searches for become part of the joy of travel.

Finally, there is one type of accommodation search that deserves a special mention. This is when the accommodation *itself* becomes the central part of one's journey. There are focal points when one needs to stop traveling in order to rest, study, and plan, as previously mentioned, for two to three weeks or even a month. In these cases, finding proper lodging for a long period is crucial in allowing oneself to truly rest and recompose. These places of long rest end up being quite special in one's journey, because one *lives*, in the full sense of the word, in the foreign country. Apart from having to learn how the country's systems work (the process of renting an apartment for three weeks in Beijing is quite a skill-acquiring task!), he also develops a deeper knowledge of the everyday life in the country, because he stays in one place and experiences life as a local.

Planning

It is impossible to plan in advance a journey that lasts for years. Even if it were possible, it would defeat the purpose, because long-term travel can only be planned generally, with broad brushstrokes. One may decide he needs, say, six months to explore China and then choose the specific regions that he will explore. However, he cannot know how long he will stay in each place—whether he will want to stay longer in a specific region or town or village because it ended up being special (or dense with attractions and things to do), or whether it was a bad choice and he need not linger there longer. Thus, every created itinerary is always tentative, and one may later readapt it in light of his explorations. The first tentative itinerary for the exploration of a country is based on many things as we saw in Addendum I. This tentative itinerary is continually changing in the light of one's experiences in a country. This also holds true for the planned itinerary of whole continents and, of course, for the world as a whole.

Regular planning is a constant activity during a world-journey. We may divide planning into three categories: current country, next country, and the rest of the journey. *Current-country planning* is the ongoing adaptation of the exploration of the country in which one happens to be. This consists mainly of adapting the preplanned tentative itinerary in the light of the new understanding of the country gained thus far. One may decide to skip a few of the places he was planning to visit, add a few others, change the mode of travel (say, use more taxis than buses if the latter have turned out to be unreliable).

While one explores a country, he must simultaneously prepare for the next one. This is the *next-country planning*. If the traveler does not do this, a hiatus will appear at the end of the exploration of the present country, since he has to spend a few days or even a week to plan the next country. It is imperative that no time is lost for preparation and planning, unless of course a long rest period has been preplanned for the end of the exploration of the present country. One must study the history and the culture of the next country and select the relevant guidebooks in order to determine the route, the entry point, and the travel mode with which one will enter the country (very important), and then the main mode of travel. It may be wise, especially if the present country is a big one, to leave the preoccupation with the next country until the end of one's exploration of the present country, so that one's studies of the present and next countries do not intermingle, and so that one may delve deeper, unencumbered by future planning, into the experiences of the country in which he happens to be. Occasionally, when many attractions happen to be near the borders, as is the case in the Patagonia region of Chile and Argentina, a simultaneous exploration of two countries might be necessary in order to save time and also in order to create a harmonious route. At other times, two neighboring countries might have similar attractions (say the Amazon rainforest that is shared by many countries) or even cultural events, and one may need to choose well in advance in which of the two he will experience something. In other cases (say, China or Germany), when one might decide to enter the country twice at two different points (in order to visit other bordering countries), what is to be explored in the two distinct visits must be carefully delineated in advance.

Finally, we have the third part of planning, which concerns the *planning for the rest of the journey*. This, of course, happens (and ought to happen) every now and then, usually during long rest periods or periods devoted to study and planning. There is always "the rest of the journey" that one must regularly rethink by taking into account how one has already moved and what one has learned from one's travels up to that moment. For example, when one has made a tentative itinerary for, say, Latin America, his decisions were based on his studies, his previous knowledge (or prejudices), and the way he evaluated the region's highlights. He may have included Venezuela and Argentina, and excluded Paraguay and Bolivia. Yet, after further study, interaction with other travelers, and a better understanding gained from months of traveling in other parts of Latin America, one may decide to add a new country and therefore replan the rest of the journey. A most important element of the constant replanning of the rest of the journey is *the reevaluation of one's total duration of the journey*. After two years of travel, a constant theme slowly becomes apparent: One is constantly way off in one's calculation of the time needed to explore an area. It seems that one needs to first travel around almost half the world in order to appreciate the *true* size of the planet. Even though the basic realization that the world is huge (Chapter II) comes quite early in the journey, the actual magnitude of this hugeness becomes apparent much later, after one has repeatedly miscalculated the Earth's size.

During the important moments of replanning the rest of the journey, the traveler, in effect, creates his wise-line around the world, his unique path out of a million possible. This unique world route, this personal line of global exploration, becomes the uniquely carved imprint of the traveler's personal choices, philosophy, tastes, and so on, on the globe itself. It is because of the *unalterable*, once-and-forever nature of this personal and unique route that every planning of *the rest of the journey* entails an immense sense of responsibility, and also an unavoidable element of sacrifice. One soon realizes that a significant part of the world will remain forever outside one's exploration and that, although it is always possible to do a second journey around the world in order to visit what one has left behind, this is unlikely to happen!

Study

There can be no long-term travel without *serious* and *systematic* study. Study is the *sifter* through which all experiences pass in order to become meaningful, as well as the *foundation* on which our understanding of the new will be built. It is also a necessary prerequisite for the practical necessity of forming an itinerary of exploration. Without study, a traveler is blindly drifting from place to place without the guiding compass of understanding.

Although study must definitely begin before any long-term journey so that one may form an overall idea of one's field of exploration, it must also continue throughout the journey. Study may be divided into the study of: (a) travel books, (b) the history and customs of the countries one visits, and (c) books of general interest.

Travel books include travels guides, travelogues, and novels inspired by travel. These are necessary to help one decide *where* to go, *how* to go, and *how long* to stay in each place. Such books help one *evaluate* countries, places, landscapes, and cultural events in order to create a tentative highlights list (see Addendum I). Travel guides, written by people who have usually explored a place at a much greater magnification than the traveler, are basically depositories of knowledge about countries and places. This knowledge, gathered over decades by many travelers, helps one choose the most interesting and important places worth visiting in a country. No itinerary can be planned without serious study of at least two guidebooks about a country—although nowadays, with the internet and ebooks, most paper books may be dispensed with altogether.

Equally important are books about the countries and cultures one visits—their flora and fauna, their history, archaeology, the character of the nations, and their traditions. No country exists in a vacuum. Every country has a centuries-old historical and cultural development that is related to other nearby or faraway cultures, plus hundreds of customs and unique mores that one must try to learn. These types of books may occasionally be augmented by travelogues or even novels by native writers or foreigners who have lived in the country. No true understanding of the Mayan or Inca civilizations is possible if one has not read in advance about these ancient civilizations, the way they were destroyed by the invading Spaniards, and how they then evolved into the modern states of Mexico, Guatemala, Bolivia, and Peru. Similarly, no true understanding of the South Pacific is possible without knowing something about its tribal past, the way Europeans created the artificial modern states we know today, and the way Christian missionaries forever altered the indigenous cultures. The same, of course, applies to the whole of Africa.

Finally, a world-traveler needs to further his overall education while he travels, just as he would have done if he were sedentary. He must expand his horizons by studying a number of different subjects: religion, so that he may better understand how societies function within their belief systems; geography, so that he may better understand the various climatic regions of the world, their topography, and natural features, as well as the relations between the various human cultures; general history, so that he may delve deeper into every culture; biology and social anthropology, so that he may learn about the living organisms of the planet, and also about the various indigenous tribes one may come across in places like Latin America or Africa. Then there are other fields, such as art, music, science, economics, and politics that help one better understand each place and the world in general. One must even, to some degree, follow current events worldwide, in order to stay in touch with the world at large and to be able to understand the changes that are currently happening in any country.

This is one of the main reasons that, probably, the best age for someone to undertake an around-the-world journey is after the age of 35, when one has sufficient life experience and also knowledge in a number of different fields. A 20-year-old may attempt a long-term journey of six months or even a year, but if he decides to do a multi-year journey around the world, he will end up missing a lot of things due to his insufficient education and life experiences.

Errands

Errands, like it or not, end up becoming part of travel. While one walks about trying to find a laundromat to wash and iron his clothes, or a cobbler to repair his shoes, or to buy a specific item such as an anti-itch lotion, in effect he is forced to interact in a more *practical* fashion with the foreign culture. Errands thus allow the traveler to approach the "everyday life" of a place from another angle. These little practical things, which are many (see a typical list below), also bring one in contact with the services, business practices, and overall "systems" in a country—things that are often invisible when one moves from place to place but does not live in the country. The running of errands may thus be considered a substitute for actually working or living in a place. Furthermore, the *form* of interactions with the foreign culture when one runs errands is usually of a very different character than when one simply travels. This immensely enriches one's travels, which offsets any annoyance of having to run errands.

A sample list of the various errands of a world-traveler:

Simple errands
    (1) Buying clothes, shoes, toiletries, etc.
    (2) Choosing the best local telecommunication card for one's cell phone
    (3) Finding an internet cafe or Wi-Fi spot
    (4) Renting a car

Medium errands
    (1) Finding a laundromat to wash and iron clothes
    (2) Repairing shoes, suitcase, camera, etc.
    (3) Photocopying and binding one's diary before sending the original one back home
    (4) Finding a boatman and negotiating for a day's boat trip

Complicated errands
  (1) Going to many travel agencies, getting offers about different types of tours/airplane tickets/excursions, evaluating them, and choosing the best
  (2) Organizing a three-day trip to explore a region with a taxi/driver/boat-man/guide
  (3) Getting a visa for a difficult country like Iran, while you are in Uzbekistan.

Rest

Finally, there is Rest—with a capital R. While running errands or planning and studying, one is not actually resting (although a relaxing read might occasionally be part of resting). Everything we examined until now is some form of work. In this sense, we may actually divide what the traveler does into just two categories: work and rest. We are not just talking about the rest necessary for rejuvenation and unwinding every week. Longer rest periods are necessary every few months. Without the regular weekly rests and the longer ones, travel becomes mechanical, without fully focused senses able to absorb the surroundings.

But by rest, we mean something more than just abstinence from travel. Long-term travel turns out to be very demanding of the mind and psyche as a whole. As we saw in Chapter II, the traveler must not only digest, absorb, and assimilate all the new experiences, but must also integrate them. Rest periods create the necessary extra time for integration to become possible. Rest is the indispensable element that allows travel to become *transformative*. The most important transformational processes happen during the periods when the physical and mental apparatuses are left unencumbered to act upon the gathered material. Rest then is much more than simple resting. It is an indispensable part of the process and mechanism by which travel furthers one's personal growth.

AUTHOR'S ITINERARY

Author's Itinerary

Regions	Country	Wks	Wks Expl
North America	USA	24	17
North America	Canada	2	2
Central America	Mexico	6	4
Central America	Belize	1	1
Central America	Guatemala	2	2
Central America	Honduras	1	1
Central America	Costa Rica	7	1.5
South America	Venezuela	2	2
South America	Brazil	7	6
South America	Uruguay	0.5	0.5
South America	Argentina	7.5	5
South America	Chile	4	4
South America	Bolivia	4	3
South America	Peru	4	4
South America	Ecuador	2	2
South America	Galápagos (Ecuador)	1.5	1.5
South America	(Chile – Santiago)	5	–
Oceania	Easter Island	1	1
Oceania	French Polynesia	2.5	2.5
Oceania	Cook Islands	1	0.5
Oceania	Samoa	3	3
Oceania	Tonga	0.5	0.5
Oceania	Fiji	8	5
Oceania	Solomon Islands	3	3
Australasia	New Zealand	13	5.5
Australasia	Australia	14	10
Maritime SE Asia	Papua New Guinea	4	4
Maritime SE Asia	Indonesia (I)	8	8
Maritime SE Asia	Malaysia	2.5	1
Maritime SE Asia	Singapore	1	1
Maritime SE Asia	Indonesia (II) – Bali	4	9*
Maritime SE Asia	Philippines	3.5	2.5
Maritime SE Asia	(Indonesia – N. Sulawesi)	9	–
East & North Asia	Taiwan	4	3
East & North Asia	Japan	8	7
East & North Asia	South Korea	1	1
East & North Asia	Russia	4	2.5
East & North Asia	Mongolia	2.5	2.5
East & North Asia	China (I)	13	9
East & North Asia	Hong Kong / Macau (China)	1.5	1.5

Regions	Country	Wks	Wks Expl
Southeast Asia	Laos	1.5	1.5
	Vietnam	2	2
	Cambodia	1.5	1.5
	Thailand	11	6
	Burma	3.5	2.5
South Asia	India	14	12
	Tibet (I)	3	1
	Nepal	2	2
Central Asia (Silk Road)	China (II)	5.5	14.5*
	Tibet (II)	2	3*
	Kyrgyzstan	1.5	1.5
	Uzbekistan	3	1.5
	Iran	2.5	2.5
Middle East	United Arab Emirates	4	2
	Oman	1	1
	Cyprus	18	2
	Egypt	2.5	2.5
Africa	Ethiopia	2.5	2.5
	Tanzania	1	1
	South Africa	9	5.5
	Cameroon	2	2
	Benin	1	1
	Togo	0.5	0.5
	Burkina Faso	0.5	0.5
	Mali	2.5	2
	Morocco	4.5	4.5
Europe	Spain	4.5	3
	France	12	9
	Belgium	0.5	0.5
	Holland	1	1
	Germany (I)	1.5	1.5
	Czech Republic	0.5	0.5
	Austria	2	1
	Germany (II)	2	3.5*
	Switzerland	1	1
	Italy	8.5	7
	Greece	8.5	8.5

Total:
6 years, 6 months

Notes on the Author's Itinerary

1. The countries are listed in the order in which I visited them. Each country is followed by the total weeks (Wks) of my visit and the total weeks of exploration (Wks Expl). I made this distinction to illustrate the true exploration time, eliminating rest, errands, and planning weeks.

2. The division of regions, although geographical, has a personal touch.

3. For countries that I visited on two separate occasions, the total exploration days after the second visit are marked with an asterisk (*).

4. Although the Galápagos Islands and Easter Island are not independent countries, I consider them destinations in their own right, due to their remoteness and their different history from their mother country. The same applies to Hong Kong and Macau.

5. Tibet is meant to denote the Tibetan culture rather than the country, which is occupied by China. Tibet (I) is Ladakh in India, and Tibet (II) is the Amdo region in China, both of which are predominantly Tibetan.

6. On two occasions, countries are in parentheses: At the end of my travels in South America, I had to backtrack to Santiago, Chile, in order to fly to Easter Island. I stayed in Santiago for five weeks to rest and plan my travels in the South Pacific. In the Philippines, I experienced an intense episode of accumulated fatigue and backtracked to my favorite country in the region, Indonesia, in order to have a much needed rest of two months there.

7. My four-month-long stay in Cyprus was due to my younger brother's sudden death.

8. Many important places that I had skipped, for example the United Kingdom, Scandinavia, most of Eastern Europe, and a big part of the Middle East, I had visited earlier in my life. I skipped Central Africa because, at the time, there were ongoing conflicts in many areas, the region had no tourist infrastructure—thus turning every exploration into a "mission"—and, finally, because I felt enervated.

Index of Quotations

CHAPTER I: DESTINATION EARTH

p. 16   Lao Tzu, Tao Te Ching, 64-2.

p. 17   Potts, Rolf. 2016. *Vagabonding: An Uncommon Guide to the Art of Long-Term World Travel*. New York: Random House, p. 5.

p. 23   Elytis, Odysseas. 1980. *Axion Esti*. Athens: Ikaros, p. 39. Author's translation.

CHAPTER II: WORLD TRAVEL

p. 44   McGuire, William, Herbert Read, Michael Fordham, and Gerhard Adler, eds. 1953-1983. *The Collected Works of C.G. Jung*, Bollingen Series 20. New York and Princeton: Princeton University Press, vol. 7, paragraph 409.

p. 48   Rangdrol, Shabkar Tsogdruk. 1994. *The Life of Shabkar: The Autobiography of a Tibetan Yogin*. Matthieu Ricard, translator. Albany, New York: SUNY Press, p. 37.

p. 56   Ghose, Sri Aurobindo. 2009. *Savitri* (Book II: The Book of the Traveler of the Worlds, Canto V: The Godheads of the Little Life). Pondicherry: Sri Aurobindo Ashram Trust, p. 162, line 400.

CHAPTER III: A NEW PHILOSOPHY OF TRAVEL

p. 72   Frankl, Viktor E. 2006. *Man's Search for Meaning*. Boston: Beacon Press, p. 138.

p. 77   Ghose, Sri Aurobindo. 2001. *The Synthesis of Yoga* (Introduction, Chapter II: The Three Steps of Nature). Pondicherry: Sri Aurobindo Ashram Trust, p. 11.

p. 77   Zweig, Stefan. 2010. *Journeys*. London: Hesperus Press Limited, p. 67.

p. 84   Ghose, Sri Aurobindo. 2001. *The Life Divine* (Book I, Chapter XII: Delight of Existence: The Solution). Pondicherry: Sri Aurobindo Ashram Trust, p. 118.

p. 86   Ghose, Sri Aurobindo. 2009. *Savitri* (Book VI: The Book of Fate, Canto II: The Way of Fate and the Problem of Pain). Pondicherry: Sri Aurobindo Ashram Trust, p. 456, line 678.

p. 92   Sophocles. *Oedipus at Colonus*. George Theodorides, translator. http://www.poetry intranslation.com/PITBR/Greek/Colonus.htm (Retrieved on April 17th, 2016).

p. 96   Steindl-Rast, David. 'Fullness and Emptiness: Thanksgiving'. http://www.grateful ness.org/resource/fullness-and-emptiness/ (Retrieved on April 17th, 2016).

p. 102   Merrell-Wolff, Franklin. 1994. *Experience and Philosophy: A Personal Record of Transformation and a Discussion of Transcendental Consciousness, Philosophy of Consciousness Without an Object*. Albany, New York: State University of New York Press, p. 398, Aphorism 36.

CHAPTER IV: PARALLELS BETWEEN A TRAVEL-JOURNEY AND OUR LIFE'S- JOURNEY

p. 107   Ghose, Sri Aurobindo. 2001. *The Life Divine* (Book I, Chapter I: The Human Aspiration), Pondicherry: Sri Aurobindo Ashram Trust, p. 6, paragraph 3.
p. 107   Frankl, Viktor E. 1985. *Man's Search for Meaning*. New York: Pocket Books, p. 143.

CHAPTER V: WORLD CITIZEN

p. 123   Laertius, Diogenes. 3rd Century AD. *Lives and Opinions of Eminent Philosophers* (Book VI, 61).
p. 124   Seneca. 1970. *De Otio*, 4.1, in Seneca Moral Essays V.2. John W. Basore, translator. Cambridge, MA: Harvard University Press, p. 187.
p. 124   Taylor, Thomas. 1822. *From Political Fragments of Archytas and other ancient Pythagoreans (Hierocles)*. https://en.wikisource.org/wiki/Political_fragments_of_Archytas_and_other_ancient_Pythagoreans/How_we_ought_to_conduct_ourselves_towards_our_kindred (Retrieved on April 17th, 2016).
p. 125   Nussbaum, Martha. 1994. "Patriotism and Cosmopolitanism", *Boston Review*: (October). http://www.bostonreview.net/martha-nussbaum-patriotism-and-cosmopolitanism (Retrieved on April 17th, 2016).
p. 128   Gibran, Khalil. 1963. *The Prophet* (On Clothes). New York: A. Knopf, p. 35.